WITNESS TO THE FAITH

Cardinal Newman on the
Teaching Authority of the Church

DUQUESNE STUDIES: THEOLOGICAL SERIES 10

1621-981

WITNESS TO THE FAITH

Cardinal Newman on the

Teaching Authority of the Church

by

GARY LEASE

Preface by Heinrich Fries

DUQUESNE UNIVERSITY PRESS
Pittsburgh, Pennsylvania 15219

DUQUESNE STUDIES: THEOLOGICAL SERIES

HENRY J. KOREN, S.T.D., *Editor*

Volume One—*Albert Dondeyne*, FAITH AND THE WORLD. xi and 324 pages. Second impression. $5.00.

Volume Two—*Peter Schoonenberg*, GOD'S WORLD IN THE MAKING. ix and 207 pages. Second impression. $3.95.

Volume Three—*Leonard J. Swidler, editor*, SCRIPTURE AND ECUMENISM. vii and 197 pages. $4.95.

Volume Four—*William H. van de Pol*, ANGLICANISM IN ECUMENICAL PERSPECTIVE. v and 293 pages. $6.75.

Volume Five—*John H. Walgrave*, PERSON AND SOCIETY. 182 pages. $4.25.

Volume Six—*Bertrand van Bilsen*, THE CHANGING CHURCH. 433 pages. $7.95.

Volume Seven—*John Heijke*, AN ECUMENICAL LIGHT ON THE RENEWAL OF RELIGIOUS COMMUNITY LIFE. TAIZE. 212 pages. Second impression. $4.50.

Volume Eight—*Heinrich Fries*, BULTMANN-BARTH AND CATHOLIC THEOLOGY. Translated by Leonard Swidler. 182 pages. $4.50.

Volume Nine—*Herman A. Fiolet*, ECUMENICAL BREAKTHROUGH. Translated by Emmanuel Levinas. 475 pages. $9.95.

© 1971 Copyright, Gary Lease

Library of Congress Catalog number: LC #71-156237.

ISBN-0-8207-0135-1

Filmset, printed and bound in the Republic of Ireland
by Irish University Press, Shannon.

'WE HAVE LOST A GREAT WITNESS TO THE FAITH'

—Cardinal Manning at the
funeral of Cardinal Newman

ACKNOWLEDGMENTS

This study was originally offered as a doctoral dissertation to the Faculty of Theology at the University of Munich. The concluding chapter 15 was not a part of that thesis and was written specifically for this publication.

Many people were instrumental in the achievement of this work. In particular my gratitude is due to: Fritz Burns, whose generous aid, over such a long period, made my study at the University of Munich possible; Rev. C. Stephen Dessain, Director of the Newman Archives at the Birmingham Oratory, who by continuous assistance and the sharing of his hard-gained knowledge played a major role in my unravelling the mystery of Newman's unpublished letters and papers; Prof. Heinrich Fries, one of Germany's leading figures in Newman scholarship, who as second reader of the completed thesis allowed me to profit from his rich experience; and finally Prof. Emeritus Michael Schmaus, my thesis director, who originally suggested this theme and whose patience saw this study through to the end.

It is said that behind every man's effort there is a woman; in this instance that is very true. It was my wife, Patricia, whose strength, always behind me, fortified me to the end. This book is as much hers as it may be mine.

G. L.

CONTENTS

ABBREVIATIONS

1. Newman's Works:

Ang. Diff.	*Difficulties of Anglicans*
Apol.	*Apologia pro Vita sua*
Arians	*Arians of the Fourth Century*
Ath. Trans.	*Select Treatises of Saint Athanasius*
Consult. Faith.	*On Consulting the Faithful in Matters of Doctrine*
Devel.	*An Essay on the Development of Christian Doctrine*
Dis. Arg.	*Discussions and Arguments*
Ess. C.H.	*Essays Critical and Historical*
Flanagan	*An Unpublished Paper on the Development of Doctrine*
Gramm.	*An Essay in Aid of a Grammar of Assent*
Hist. Sketch.	*Historical Sketches*
Letters	*Letters and Correspondence of J. H. Newman during his Life in the English Church*
Letters and Diaries	*The Letters and Diaries of J. H. Newman*
Mix. Cong.	*Discourses to Mixed Congregations*
Orat.	*The Newman Private Papers*
P.P.	*Parochial and Plain Sermons*
Plum.	*The Plummer Private Papers*
Pres. Pos.	*Lectures on the Present Position of Catholics in England*
Tr. Theol. Ecc.	*Tracts Theological and Ecclesiastical*
U.S.	*Fifteen Sermons Preached before the University of Oxford*
V.M.	*The Via Media of the Anglican Church*

2. Other Works:

L.Th.K.	*Lexikon für Theologie und Kirche*
O.D.C.C.	*Oxford Dictionary of the Christian Church*
Ward	W. Ward, *The Life of John Henry Cardinal Newman*

For bibliographical details of these and all publications referred to in the present work, see Bibliography, pp. 144ff.

PREFACE

Doctrinal authority in the Church and its relation to faith is today very much in the forefront of theological discussion. A *historical* investigation of the problem—as it evolved, for example, in the life and work of John Henry Newman—does not at all mean a flight from the present: it offers the student of today the great service of suggesting lines of orientation. There is no problem touching on faith or on the Church so new that it emerges today for the very first time; no answer sought today for which there are no antecedents. The search for answers cannot afford to ignore history, to disdain what has been worked out and thought out in the past. History, rightly approached, does not reveal simply how a thing *was*; it reveals how it *is,* how it acts and reacts, how its manifold aspects converge and interact.

For this reason *Witness to the Faith*—apart from the great interest it will have for admirers and students of Newman—makes a valuable contribution towards solution of a problem that exercises Christian minds today. This is so, first, because Newman as theologian is extraordinarily topical—we are only now coming to realize fully how much he has to offer contemporary theology—and secondly because the Church, the magisterium, faith, conscience and freedom are among the themes to which he devoted a lifetime of theological reflection. Newman spared himself no pains to render them a genuine and credible formulation. Hence the importance of considering the answers that his faith and thought can offer to contemporary problems.

Gary Lease, author of the present work, is well acquainted with the writings of Cardinal Newman, their subsequent history and the present state of Newman studies. His comments and judgments are well-founded and always to the point. Especially to be singled out is his aptitude for exact and succinct interpretation which, going beyond mere words and seeking out the underlying facts, has overlooked nothing of importance. That he gives special attention to particular works of Newman is entirely justified. Newman's great historical work on the Arian controversy has not until now been accorded the attention it deserves, and its influence on his theology has been neglected. This is, then, an added merit of Dr Lease's book, that it pays special attention to this early work of Newman's. The author is also to be congratulated for his synoptic view of the various elements in Newman's treatment of the theme in question, and for his historical and genetic analysis of this theme as it unfolded in Newman's life and thought. We are shown a clearly articulated development as it emerged against a background of unchanging principles. Newman's statements after the First Vatican Council were a kind of culmination and summary of his theological reflections on this theme. At the same time they sounded a note of alarm in a situation not unlike our own today. Dr Lease lays particular stress on this point.

With this work Gary Lease shows himself at once a Newman scholar and a theologian intensely committed to and engaged in the challenges of the present.

Munich, 4 March 1969   Heinrich Fries

INTRODUCTION

There is clear unrest in the theological world of today. Leading experts are pointing out that one of the major reasons for this is the uncertain position of the magisterium of the Church. Some authors even view the situation as much more alarming and report the Church to be in a state of 'disintegration'. Gregory Baum remarks that 'there can be no doubt that some doctrinal positions taught by the highest ecclesiastical magisterium in the past no longer express present-day teaching'.[1] At the root of this disturbance is a confrontation over the role of authority in the Church of Christ. Yet at this very moment, and for the last hundred years, the status of authority in the Roman Catholic Church has undergone vast changes.

Since the Reformation, authority, both temporal and spiritual, had been used—mainly by the papacy—to enforce an ecclesiastical unity thought to have been made necessary by the splitting of the Christian West at the break-up of the High Middle Ages. During the nineteenth century this battle was thought to have been won through the concentration of authority—and thus unity—in the hands of the Roman popes.[2] But since then a World War has laid the globe waste; another Council has been held to reassess the

1. 'The Magisterium in a Changing Church' in *Concilium* 1 (1967) 34. See also *National Catholic Reporter,* Kansas City, 3 (1967) 23 August, p. 10.
2. See M. Laros, 'Laie und Lehramt in der Kirche' in *Hochland* 37 (1939/40) 46. E. T. O'Dwyer, *Cardinal Newman and the Encyclical Pascendi,* London, 1908, p. ix: 'The Pope and the Bishops legislate; the laity obey. If one is a Catholic, he believes these things, and if he does, he must hold with the Pope, who simply protests against an attempt to reverse the order which Christ has established.' For development of this thought in the nineteenth century, see Y. Congar, 'L'ecclésiologie, de la Révolution française au Concile du Vatican, sous le signe de l'affirmation de l'autorité' in *L'Ecclésiologie au XIXe siècle,* Paris, 1960, pp. 77–114.

Church's position in accordance with Newman's sanguine hopes;[3] a decree on religious liberty has reinforced the role of the individual conscience in its religious and moral decisions. In short, the milieu in which the authority of the Church functioned in the nineteenth century has changed fundamentally, and thus the very concept of authority itself. Yet to attempt to develop the concept of authority in the Church, especially in the area of the magisterium, is to invite attack from many corners.[4]

This treatise is dedicated to the proposition that such a theological development must take place in the area of the magisterial activity of the Church. It is not an easy area to work in and it has received added urgency through the widely publicized leave-taking of Charles Davis from formal union in the Roman Catholic Church. His is a personal tragedy, the scope of which is far too deep for this study; but it does accentuate the unrest and unclarity surrounding the problem of magisterial authority in the Church: a man who was for years one of England's most respected theologians and a *peritus* at the Second Vatican Council does not take such a step as a whim of the moment. Indeed, he himself says it was the result of a long period of study and meditation, cresting finally on the fact, for him, that he could not experience 'the papal authority as a living doctrinal centre, focusing, representing and sanctioning the mind of the Church'.[5] And this is so for many more of the faithful who are not in a position to make their feelings known as publicly as Charles Davis was. But the problem is there:

> For many people today dogma appears to express a lack of liberty which contradicts man's dignity; for them dogma is loaded with historical memories of inquisition, condemnation,

3. See J. H. Newman to A. Plummer, 3 April 1871, cited in F. L. Cross, *John Henry Newman*, p. 170: '. . . looking at early history, it would seem as if the Church moved on to the perfect truth by various successive declarations, alternately in contrary directions, and thus perfecting, completing, supplying each other . . . but let us be patient, let us have faith, and a new Pope, and a reassembled Council may trim the boat.'

4. See J. McKenzie, *Authority in the Church*, p. 18: 'One suspects that theological development of the theory of authority is regarded as an attack upon authority, subtle or open. Statements on the idea and use of authority quite often recall the members of the Church to an ideal of obedience which was formed in the sixteenth century or earlier. This one area, it appears, is excepted from the general law of theological development. One would like to know the basis of this exception . . .'

5. See Charles Davis, 'Why I left the Roman Catholic Church' in *The Observer Review*, 1 January 1967, p. 1.

exile, persecution, burning and violence done to the human conscience. It is not merely one or the other particular dogma, but the very fact that there is such a thing as dogma that constitutes for many an almost insuperable barrier that bars their access to the Gospel. To them there appears to exist a vast gulf between the glad tidings of the freedom of the children of God and dogma.[6]

It is not just an isolated phenomenon, concentrating itself in pockets of disgruntled church members and articulating itself in learned journals and obtuse public addresses. On the contrary, it is the general appearance of this feeling with which we have to deal; it is one of those thought patterns which pervade the new world we live in as simply belonging to that world, and a call to the past is not going to satisfy this feeling:

> Today we are in another period of reformation. We are in it because the theological doctrines and religious forms we have inherited from the past have reached the end of their usefulness . . . People now realize that they can take doctrine as symbolically as they please . . . their complaint focuses on the failure of the Church to live up to its own stated ideals. Many people who drop out of the Church today do so not because they find its teaching unintelligible but because it has abandoned its role as the conscience troubler and moral avant-garde of society . . . They will drop out because they believe the churches are no longer fitting representatives of that message . . .[7]

Thus one of America's leading theologians. And where does he lay the cause of the problem? 'The most crucial issue, for the future of the churches themselves, has to do with the nature of churchly authority.'[8] This crisis is seen as so serious by some that they would speak of a new reformation of Christianity.[9]

The fundamental upheavals responsible for this situation are not altogether clear, but one major component in its structure is becoming more and more obvious: our increasing experience that truth, in any form, is tinged deeply with relativity. The

6. W. Kasper, 'The Relationship between Gospel and Dogma' in *Concilium* 1 (1967) 73.
7. Harvey Cox, 'Revolt in the Church' in *Playboy,* January 1967, p. 129.
8. *Ibid.*
9. *Ibid.*, p. 211.

experience of the last fifty years, both technologically and socially, has brought home to us the crushing experience that as human beings we are doomed to a knowledge of ourselves, of our world and of our relationships to these two givens which is at best determined by an unknowable amount of historical qualifications; in other words, we are today fully aware—if we had not been so before—that, as human beings, absolute knowledge is a historical impossibility. Such awareness can be very healthy in leading us to a fuller and deeper understanding and appreciation of the place the revealed religion we call Christianity has in our historical existence. But it has its dangers, too. It can lead the other way, towards a complete disinterestedness, towards a relativity of truth which says: since I can know nothing absolutely, I can know nothing at all. And this ever-present danger adds to the necessity for a study such as this.

This study, then, is not only dedicated to the conviction that it *should* be undertaken, but that it *must* be undertaken, in the hope that, no matter how small it may be, some clarity may thus be introduced into the chaos which today surrounds the magisterial activities of the Church.

The focus of this study therefore is the teaching function of the Church as seen in its fundament: what is the basis and justification for a teaching function in a Church of Christ? It will be studied in the light of the thought and development of John Henry Newman,[10] and this for two reasons: Newman is without doubt one of the most brilliant and influential thinkers of our times. Due to his studies in the Fathers and his own role in nineteenth-century theology he has often been called the Father of our times.[11] But his importance for the Church beyond the field of scholarly theology has also been recognized; Pope Paul VI has even called the Second Vatican Council 'Newman's Council'.[12] At the same

10. For his life, see W. Ward, *The Life of John Henry Cardinal Newman*, 2 volumes, London, 1912; written by the son of one of Newman's most stormy adversaries during his later life, it presents a theologically orientated view of his life and work. For a more modern presentation, see M. Trevor, *Newman*, 2 volumes, London, 1961; for a more detailed look at Newman's Anglican life and the influences which formed his thought and character, see M. Ward, *Young Mr. Newman*, London, 1948.

11. See M. Laros, 'Kardinal Newman and das "neue" Dogma' in *Die Neue Ordnung* 5 (1951) 6; also H. F. Davis, 'Le rôle et l'apostolat de la hiérarchie et du laicat dans la théologie de l'Eglise chez Newman' in *L'Ecclésiologie au XIXe siècle*, Paris, 1960, p. 329.

12. AAS 55 (1963) 1025.

time, however, we find that the very problem we are treating has received scant attention from scholars probing the works of Newman. This is most likely due to the vast amount of material he left behind and the very complexity of his life and writings: it is most difficult to avoid splitting his thought together with his life along the lines of his leaving the Anglican Church, where he spent exactly half of his life, and his joining the Catholic Church. As we will attempt to show, however, there is a unity in his thought which, despite the lack of a prominent sense for systematization, stretches from the one end of his life to the other.[13]

As J. M. Cameron has put it: 'We may say that all his writing, not excluding the *Grammar,* was the fulfilment of his deeply felt and continuously lived vocation as an inquirer into and a teacher of the mysteries of faith.'[14] This connecting link in his work is to be met with, in lesser or greater degree, in every event and work of his life. These two—his life and his work—were inextricably intertwined: to understand his work one must have knowledge of his life, and to understand his life one must know his work.[15] This connecting link—inquiring and teaching—is really nothing more than the great task of translating the truths of Christianity into the concrete situation of God's meeting with the individual.[16] It is precisely this characteristic of Newman's life and work which makes him a singularly apposite subject of our inquiry: all his life he was concerned with nothing other than the problem of a religion of revelation—in this case the Christian Church—and its attempt to proclaim this revelation to mankind.

But there are dangers. H. Tristram points out that '. . . through a long succession of years' he has read widely 'in the literature connected with Newman' and has acquainted himself 'with his papers and unpublished writing—letters, notes, memoranda, inchoate books'. This experience has 'impressed indelibly upon his mind one momentous conclusion that much of what has been written about him is purely fanciful and without any solid basis in facts'.[17] No one can say better what Newman wants to say than

13. See H. Fries, 'J. H. Newmans Beitrag zum Verständnis der Tradition' in *Die mündliche Ueberlieferung,* Munich, 1957, p. 103.
14. *John Henry Newman,* London, 1963, p. 8.
15. See H. Tristram, 'On Reading Newman' in *John Henry Newman: Centenary Essays,* London, 1945, pp. 227, 239.
16. See O. Karrer, 'John Henry Newman' in *Hochland* 40 (1947/48) 518.
17. 'Cardinal Newman and Baron von Hügel' in *The Dublin Review* 509 (1966) 296–7.

Newman himself; the attempt to recast it and expand upon it often proves frustrating and impossible—if for no other reason than that of language. In this case, however, Newman was quite clear as to what he meant; he just never systematically presented it—as with a good many other subjects he confronted in his long life. Therefore this study has additional justification: the attempt to organize and cast into a whole the thoughts and workings which represented for their author a conceptual whole is not without worth. In the light of our present-day situation, as sketched above, it might prove valuable as pointing in the direction of a viable solution.

The thesis to be presented here is supported by Newman's published and unpublished works and letters; it therefore stretches over the whole of his life. This at once proves to be a strength in formulating the idea defended by this study, for one can draw on the whole of Newman's output in doing so. On the other hand it proves to be a weakness because the various expressions of this concept are seen to have been influenced by various events during his long life. However, following in general the method used by Günter Biemer,[18] it will be possible to pursue the historical development of Newman's thought and trace its changes and expansions from work to work and from the Anglican Church to the Roman Church.

The thesis itself is deceptively simple. As presented in this study it takes the following form: Newman held, right from the first work he wrote—*The Arians of the Fourth Century*—the belief that the Church, teaching in and with the authority of Christ, based its presentation of Christian doctrine on the witness of the whole Church to its faith in that doctrine. In *Arians* Newman will show this in a historical view of the fourth century and the battle within the Church at the time of the Arian heresy. His ideas will mature in the 1830s as he comes to develop his concept of the infallibility of the Church; he will begin to emphasize one pole of the witness the Church gives to its faith. With the approach of his leave-taking from the Church of England he will increase this accentuation, until we meet the exaggerated emphasis he lays upon the authority

18. In his fine study, *Die Lehre von der Tradition nach John Henry Newman*, diss. masch., Tübingen, 1959; this has since appeared in book form: *Ueberlieferung und Offenbarung*, Freiburg, 1961, and in English translation: *Newman on Tradition*, New York, 1967.

and infallibility of the pope—and thus, implicitly, of the hierarchy as a whole—in the matter of teaching and communicating true Christian doctrine which we find in his *Essay on the Development of Christian Doctrine*. By the 1850s, however, due to his own sobering personal experiences, his thoughts in this direction will be returning to a more balanced point of view, as illustrated by the now infamous *Rambler* affair. This process will be traced further in the 1860s and 70s as he wrestles with the rising problem of papal infallibility and the attendant difficulties.

At this point we hope it will become clear that Newman, in the various writings of his career, had been illustrating now one side, now another, of the organic view he in reality held all his life: 'Laity and papacy are organically related to each other. Newman had realized this during his study of the Arian crisis, and he experienced it during the Oxford Movement. This is one of the motivations which led him to Rome.'[19] Once in the Church of Rome he worked for the rest of his long life towards achieving a balanced presentation of this relationship between the people of God and the hierarchy within the one Church of Christ. It is here, at the point of authority's junction with freedom, that Newman closed the circle of his thought: 'He maintained both the authority of unity as well as the freedom of plurality.'[20] It is this aspect of Newman's thought that interests us here, but in particular in light of the question: on what basis can, and does, the Church of Christ function in a teaching capacity?

It is the firm hope of the author, and indeed the only justification for taking up this investigation, that what Newman expressed so clearly on this matter may help us to enter once more into that harmony of community within the Church which characterizes not only the doctrine of that Church but also the teaching of it.

19. Jean Guitton, *Mitbürgern der Wahrheit*, Salzburg, 1964, p. 141. This work has since appeared in English translation: *The Church and the Laity: From Newman to Vatican II*, New York, 1965. In the present study all references will be to the German edition.
20. *Ibid.*, p. 140.

I

Early Gropings

This is not a biography of Newman; such would be out of place and, besides, the capable works have already been mentioned.[1] But, as also pointed out above, a study of Newman's thought on any subject will lack a necessary element for understanding if the essential connection between his thought and life is missing. Thus, in the case presented here, a proper sketch of the life Newman was leading behind the thought being studied will be indispensable.

Despite the importance of Newman's now well-known 'conversion' at the age of fifteen,[2] it was not until 1822, when he was twenty-one years old, that Newman made any decision concerning a future life connected with the Church. It was then, after his failure in exams in the winter of 1820, that he decided to change his plans and enter upon an ecclesiastical career.[3] His election as a fellow to Oriel and the ensuing fellowship with Whately[4] confirmed him in his choice.

With his ordination as deacon in 1824, Newman took over a curacy at St Clement's, an Oxford parish. From the start he showed his interest in bringing the message of the Christian revelation to those under his care. A letter to his father at this time shows him visiting the poor of his parish, but not just the poor, for he found that those who were better off had been able to educate their

1. See Introduction, footnote 10, above.
2. *Apol.*, p. 4; see also the treatment in L. Bouyer, *Newman, his Life and Spirituality*, London, 1958, where a whole chapter effectively places this event in a proper perspective for the whole of Newman's life.
3. *Letters* I, p. 41: his father had destined him for a future in law and had entered him in 1819 at Lincoln's Inn; but, in a note in his diary—11 January 1822—he writes: 'My father this evening said I ought to make up my mind what I was to be . . . so I chose; and determined on the Church. Thank God, this is what I have prayed for' (quoted in M. Ward, *Young Mr. Newman*, p. 62).
4. Ward, *Young Mr. Newman*, p. 94.

children: 'and on that ground it is that a clergyman is more concerned with the children of the latter, though our Church certainly intended that, not only schoolmasters of the poorer children, but all schoolmasters high and low, should be under her jurisdiction'.[5] Unfortunately, he goes on, such is not the case; but it was a condition for which he felt one had to strive. He means here, of course, that education pertaining to the Church's message: the Church has, in these early thoughts of Newman, an essential task in communicating the Christian revelation to those committed to its care. Even as a deacon and curate he felt drawn to this effort; he was soon to make it more so.

In 1826 Newman accepted an offer to be one of the public tutors for Oriel College; this necessitated his giving up his curacy at St Clement's. At this time in Oxford there were two opinions as to the compatibility of a teaching office with that of a clergyman. One position held that the two were basically opposed, while the other thought it to be a question of no importance. Newman, however, struck a third position: 'To him it seemed that the office of a tutor was itself sacred—that it should involve not merely supervision of the studies of his pupils but also a true pastoral office towards them.'[6]

Here is a basic characteristic of Newman's life and work coming to surface for the first time: his devotion to the teaching office in connection with the mission of the Church; for him the functions could be equated. ' "To live and die a Fellow of Oriel" meant for him to live and die a missionary to youth.'[7] And thus he fulfilled his new office. Having assumed his duties in the Easter term of 1826, he set about them with great energy. Writing in his journal at the time, he says: 'It is my wish to consider myself as the minister of Christ. Unless I find that opportunities occur of doing spiritual good to those over whom I am placed, it will become a grave question whether I ought to continue in the tuition.'[8] This idea— that secular education could be so conducted as to become a pastoral ministry—was held by him with the greatest tenacity, and was to

<hr />

5. *Letters* I, p. 77.
6. Ward, *Young Mr. Newman,* p. 112.
7. *Ibid.,* p. 113; see also *Letters* I, pp. 79–80, where, on the occasion of his father's death, he writes in his diary: '. . . I think I shall either die within college walls, or as a missionary in a foreign land', thus effectively joining the two vocations together.
8. *Ibid.,* p. 133.

lead later to his having to give up his position as tutor. But of that we will hear later.

Along with his duties as tutor at Oriel College, he was given in 1828 the post of vicar at St Mary's, the university church in Oxford. Bishop Howley of London had already named him one of the preachers at Whitehall, and in 1831–32 he was appointed one of the University Select Preachers. Thus it is in his sermons that we can first begin to trace his thought during this early period of his life.

In 1829 Newman gave a sermon concerning submission to church authority.[9] The text he chose as the theme of his sermon is indicative:

> Put away from you crooked speech and put devious talk far from you. Let your eyes look directly forward, and your gaze be straight before you. Take heed to the path of your feet, then all your ways will be sure. Do not swerve to the right or to the left; turn your foot away from evil (Proverbs 4: 24–27).

He strikes immediately a nerve which was to serve for the rest of his life as one of his guiding principles: that of authority in the Church and of the obedience due this authority:

> At the present time, when religious unity and peace are so lamentably disregarded, and novel doctrines and new measures alone are popular, they naturally remind us of the duty of obedience to the Church.[10]

This obedience due authority in the Church of Christ is based upon another, even more profound principle in Newman's thought: the unity of the Church:

> You know time was when there was but one vast body of Christians, called the Church, throughout the world. It was found in every country where the name of Christ was named; it was everywhere governed in the same way by Bishops; it was everywhere descended from the Apostles through the line of those Bishops; and it was everywhere in perfect peace and unity together, branch with branch, all over the world.[11]

But this has all changed through the centuries; the Church is split,

9. Now to be found in *P.P.* III, n. xiv, pp. 190–205.
10. *P.P.* III, p. 190.
11. *Ibid.*, p. 191.

and there are those who would save the situation with 'vessels not of God's building'.[12] Newman then refutes the arguments of the day which would have Christians ignore rightful church authority, in order to create both a humanistic and an indifferent community joined together by good will more than by faith in Christ.[13] For Newman such action would militate against one of the basic facts of Scripture: the unity of the Church.[14] For him 'it is as direct a contradiction of Scripture to speak of more than one body as to speak of more than one Spirit'.[15] This very unity of the Church, constituted as one by Christ himself, demands that we pay the obedience due to authority within this unity. For it is not only 'our interest, our soul's interest' which demands that we remain in union with those ministers of the word and sacraments of Christ, but 'it is plainly our duty also'.[16] Even if we find those who are set above us in error, we must 'pray for them, not abandon them. If they sin against us, let not us sin against them. Let us return good for evil'.[17] The errors of particular teachers within the Church can never justify separation from the Church; this is because teaching was committed to the Church for a very different reason than that imagined by those who would do so. 'If individual teachers were infallible, there would be no need of order and rule at all.'[18] But they are not. 'If we had a living Head upon earth, such as once our Saviour was with His disciples, teaching and directing us in all things, the visible Church might *so far* be dispensed with.'[19] But we have not such a one.

Here there is a basic misunderstanding in Newman's thought, which will manifest itself much more clearly in his later *Prophetical*

12. *Ibid.*, p. 192.
13. *Ibid.*
14. This aspect of Newman's thought has been given a very thorough treatment in N. Schiffers, *Die Einheit der Kirche nach J. H. Newman*, Düsseldorf, 1956; in reference to the theme discussed here, see especially pp. 207–23, on the proclaiming Church, and pp. 236–45, on the hierarchical structure of the Church.
15. *P.P.* III, p. 193.
16. *Ibid.*, p. 198.
17. *Ibid.*; and so it was for the whole of Newman's life: R. Grosche, writing of the end of Newman's life and of the injustices he had experienced at the hands of church authorities, says: 'He never defended an action or measure which had not been approved by ecclesiastical authority. When he saw that his chosen way would not be approved by that authority, he gave it up—not resigned, but quietly hoping for the future' ('Newman und die kirchliche Autorität' in *Pilgernde Kirche*, Freiburg, 1938, p. 219).
18. *P.P.* III, p. 198.
19. *Ibid.*

Office, namely a misunderstanding of infallibility. Here infallibility is seen not as an unerring judgment on and witness to the truth or falsity of faith and morals, but as an ability to discern, penetrate and then bind the results upon those under that authority.[20] *If* such a faculty were present in the Church, then in *so far* could we dispense with the institution of the Church, i.e. the teaching office of the Church, for nothing would need to be taught. It would be immediately apprehensible, for it would be infallible. We will find this concept of infallibility still causing Newman trouble during his controversy over the development of doctrine.

But such is not the case, he goes on to say. And so: 'The whole body of Christians thus become the *trustees* of it, to use the language of the world, and, in fact, have thus age after age transmitted it down to ourselves.' Transmitted what? A form of doctrine, binding all in the unity of the Church and securing the stability of sacred truth.[21] Thus, 'Teachers have been bound to teach in one way not in another, as well as hearers to hear.'[22] Here Newman elucidates quite clearly an idea that will pervade, in varying degrees, his thought throughout the rest of his life: the interdependence of the teachers of the Church upon those whom they teach, and vice versa. For those who teach, the guiding line must be the faith in Christ as guarded and preserved through the centuries by the whole Christian community, living this faith as real; but those who guard and preserve this faith, the hearers of the Word, receive that which they are to keep whole and live in truth from the teachers of their community. It was a continual striving of Newman to strike a balance within the whole Church between these two quite different and yet quite interdependent roles.[23] This striving, of course, played a fundamental part in his determination of the teaching function of the Church. A proper understanding of this function, according to Newman, could only be achieved in a context dominated by a balance of these aspects of the Church's one mission: the proclamation of Christ.

He illustrates, further on in the same sermon, the disastrous

20. See M. J. Connolly, *Newman's Anglican Concept of the Doctrinal Authority of the Church and its Relation to Infallibility*, Rome, 1951, pp. 89–90.
21. *P.P.* III, p. 199.
22. *Ibid.*
23. See H. F. Davis, 'Le rôle et l'apostolat de la hiérarchie et du laicat dans la théologie de l'Eglise chez Newman' in *L'Ecclésiologie au XIXᵉ siècle*, Paris, 1960, p. 349.

effects of giving up submission to the proper authority in the Church: loss of the unity within the Church, the unity Newman praised so highly. 'But if every one follow his own rule of fellowship, how can there possibly be but "one body", and in what sense are those words of the Apostle to be taken?'[24] This is an important concern, and one pointing up the fundamental role played by the Church's note of unity in its teaching function. It is as *one* Church ('the whole body of Christians') that the Christian community has its mission to teach and communicate the revelation entrusted to it by Christ. Newman sings the praises of this Church-constituting unity towards the end of his sermon:

> If Christ has constituted one Holy Society (which He has done); if His Apostles have set it in order (which they did), and have expressly bidden us (as they have in Scripture) not to undo what they have begun; and if (in matter of fact) their Work so set in order and so blessed is among us this very day (as it is), and we partakers of it, it were a traitor's act in us to abandon it, an unthankful slight on those who have preserved it for so many ages, a cruel disregard of those who are to come after us, nay of those now alive who are external to it and might otherwise be brought into it. We must transmit as we have received. We did not make the Church, we may not unmake it.[25]

We may not undo the Church by usurping tasks which do not belong to us, but neither are those tasks—of teaching—able to be carried out by those entrusted with them unless upon the basis of those—the whole body of Christians—who witness to the faith given to the Church by Christ. Newman notes at the very end of his sermon that the 'happiest state of life is one in which we had not to command or direct, but *to obey solely* . . .'[26] It would be the happiest, but it is not given to all. And even those in obedience bind, by their very obedience, those to whom they owe their submission. These thoughts, sketched out here in one of Newman's early sermons, will guide us through the development of his thinking in his later works.

An interlude in Newman's scholarly work was provided by the struggle for Catholic Emancipation. It had been in the air for over

24. *P.P.* III, p. 200.
25. *Ibid.*, p. 202.
26. *Ibid.*, p. 205.

twenty years.[27] Finally, with the election in 1828 of an Irish Catholic to the House of Commons, the then prime minister, the Duke of Wellington, and his home secretary, Robert Peel, felt that Catholic Emancipation was necessary in order to avoid civil war in Ireland.[28] But Peel, having taken office committed against such a move, felt honor-bound to resign his position in Parliament and stand again for his seat. It was the seat from Oxford.

A bitter contest followed, with the various dons choosing sides for the election. The liberals, led by Hawkins, Newman's provost at Oriel, together with Pusey, were leading the campaign for Peel's re-election. But Newman swung to the other side, and supported the movement to block Peel's re-election. The motives for his move, and his joy at his success (though short-lived), are of little moment to our theme. But during this campaign he penned his thoughts on the future of the Church in a letter to his mother, and this will be germane to our topic.

The letter, dated 13 March 1829, begins with a dour description of the dangers of the age to the Church; he then goes on to say that the 'talent of the day is against the Church'.[29] The Church party, in his mind, is short on mental ability; what then, he asks, can support the Church? His answer: prejudice and bigotry. He continues:

> This is hardly an exaggeration; yet I have good meaning and one honourable to the Church. Listen to my theory. As each individual has certain instincts of right and wrong antecedently to reasoning, on which he acts—and rightly so—which perverse reasoning may supplant, which then can hardly be regained, but if regained, will be regained from a different source—from reasoning, not from nature—so, I think, has the world of men collectively. God gave them truths in His miraculous revelations, and other truths in the unsophisticated infancy of nations, scarcely less necessary and divine. These are transmitted as 'the wisdom of our ancestors', through men—many of whom cannot enter into them, or receive them themselves—still on, on, from age to age, not the less truths because many of the generations through which they are transmitted are unable to prove them, but hold them, either from pious and honest feeling (it may be), or from bigotry or from prejudice.[30]

27. O. Chadwick, *The Victorian Church* I, London, 1966, p. 9.
28. Ward, *Young Mr. Newman,* p. 154.
29. *Letters* I, p. 180.   30. *Ibid.*

Here Newman brings home his conviction that the truths with which the Church is concerned (for it is the Church which is his source of worry) are carried on not only by the proclamation of them on the part of authority, but also, and at times alone,[31] by the mass of men, the community as a whole in its role of preserving and guarding and transmitting to the future that living faith which is the foundation of the one Church.

But he still was wrestling with the problem of how to reconcile the two functions involved in this process. In 1830, in a tract written for circulation among the Oxford members of the Church Missionary Society, he reverses his position and expresses a desire for a more whole-hearted submission to church authority. As he himself says, one of his objects in writing the tract was 'to direct and strengthen the influence of the University, and thereby of the Anglican hierarchy, upon it'.[32] He felt this influence to be a necessity for the success of the society; but it 'gave great offence to the leading members of the Oxford Branch'.[33] At the next meeting Newman, who had held the office of secretary, was voted out of it.

Beginning his remarks with an account of the society until then, Newman notices that it has 'evinced little regard for the duty of church order and canonical obedience'.[34] His complaint is that, in setting up a public organization and yet professing to be a part of the Church of England and taking over a task essential to the Church, it should be more directly under the control of that Church; otherwise the tendency would be 'to make the people, not the Bishop, the basis and moving principle of her constitution'.[35] This tendency is to be seen in the fact that, in taking over such a task as that of the missions, the society has 'taken on itself a function which, not less than that of ordination, is to be considered the prerogative of the supreme rulers of the Christian Church'.[36] Newman can only view such a development with consternation, for in his eyes it is injuring the Church.

Once again we see him holding fast to his principle of unity in

31. Newman presages here an idea which later caused him much trouble in his *Rambler* article.
32. *V.M.* II, p. 3.
33. *Ibid.*, p. 4.
34. *Ibid.*, p. 10.
35. *Ibid.*, p. 11.
36. *Ibid.*

the Church, a unity cemented through the act of submission to the proper authority. It has been said that none of Newman's contemporaries did more for the cause of authority than he;[37] and this is certainly quite true, seen from one side of the ledger. Motivated by concern for the Church, he felt that, as we have just seen in our analysis of one of his sermons, any separation from the authority in the Church could only mean separation from, and injury to, the unity of the Church.[38] Remembering his close equation of the Church's missionary activity with its teaching function, we can draw the conclusion that, no matter how basic the witness of the whole community is to the teaching of the Church, it is still essential for this act of witness that it be submissive to the authority set over it.

In the meantime, Newman's activities as tutor at Oriel College were drawing to a close. In the course of the few years since his appointment to that post, he had set into action his principles, as outlined above. Together with Froude and Wilberforce he had acquired considerable influence over the students; those given to them under the tutorial scheme of college education were treated with a personal relation to their tutor, who treated them in return with the fervor befitting Newman's conviction that teaching was a sacred duty.[39] This, however, could not be tolerated by the provost, Hawkins, and various others of the college, Whately among them.[40] The problem finally came to a boil when the three tutors demanded that they be allowed to arrange the lectures for their students at their own discretion; a demand which the provost was not willing to grant. A correspondence ensued, the result being that Newman and his companions were simply denied any pupils by the provost to the end that, as their present pupils graduated, they eventually had nothing to do. They had no choice but to resign. Newman added his reason for doing so in a letter to the provost: ' . . . the mere lecturing required of me would be incompatible with due attention to that more useful private instruction, which has imparted to the office of tutor the importance of a clerical occupation.'[41]

A year and a half later, commenting on his move to a friend, he

---

37. See R. Grosche, 'Newmans Bedeutung für die Gegenwart' in *Pilgernde Kirche,* Freiburg, 1938, p. 233.
38. *V.M.* II, p. 12.
39. See Ward, *Young Mr. Newman,* p. 180; also *Letters* I, p. 137.
40. *Ibid.*
41. *Letters* I, p. 139.

says that he had 'ever considered the office pastoral, such that the tutor was entrusted with a discretionary power over his pupils'.[42] And then he tells how firm a position this view has in his thought: 'My decision, right or wrong, was made not in haste or passion, but from *long* principles; and it is immutable.'[43] We can see clearly how important a place his feeling for the teaching office of the Church occupied in his thought; he even extended it, as in this case, to the secular sphere.

From Newman's early period—before the period of the Oxford Movement—the last document which applies to our topic is another sermon, one preached at the end of 1831. In it he considers how one can follow the evangelical counsel to profess one's faith, and yet do so in an unostentatious manner. In discussing this problem he touches on the question of profession as such. For him the main form, as such basic to all acts of profession, is simple obedience to the Church: 'He who simply did what the Church bids him do (if he did no more), would witness a good confession to the world.'[44] Here he has in mind the fundamental submission essential to life within the Church: 'He does only what he is told to do; he takes no responsibility on himself.'[45]

Posts of responsibility are given in the grace of Christ to those selected for such an office. This is not everyone's task and one should not assume the responsibility of authority on one's own merits. If, Newman says, 'a man stands forth *on his own ground,* declaring himself as an individual a witness for Christ, then indeed he *is* grieving and disturbing the calm spirit given us by God'.[46] He is disrupting the unity of the whole, so very necessary in Newman's thought.

But there is a way to bear witness which avoids such ostentatious and rupturing self-witness; it is the way of community:

> God bids us unite together in one, and to shelter our personal profession under the authority of the general body. Thus . . . we show ourselves as lights to the world far more effectively than if we glimmered separately in the lone wilderness without communication with others.[47]

Thus it is, he continues, that the Church regulates our prayer and

---

42. *Ibid.,* p. 140.
43. *Ibid.*
44. *PP.* I, p. 153.

45. *Ibid.*
46. *Ibid.*
47. *Ibid.,* pp. 153–4.

liturgical life, the fasts and the feasts, the sacraments; for these are expressions of a living witness, one which acts and subsumes the very lives of those witnessing. And for Newman such a living witness is only possible in the unity of the believing community:

> I am desirous of speaking on this subject as a matter of *practice*; for I am sure, that if we wish really and in fact to spread the knowledge of the Truth, we shall do so far more powerfully as *well* as purely, by keeping together, than by witnessing one by one.[48]

But there is also a second way such a profession can take place: the 'mere ordinary manner in which any strict Christian lives'.[49] This is essentially connected to the foregoing way; it is the living witness—whether in daily life, or in the visible community of the faithful—that is important and basic to the fundamental task of the Church, the spreading of the knowledge of Christ, in which every one of the faithful partakes: 'Your *life* displays Christ without your intending it.'[50] If your faith is truly living, then you are witnessing at all times, no matter what your position in the world, no matter what you are doing. This thought, so basic to Newman's concept of the teaching function of the Church, we will meet again and again.

But we must not be misled by this thought. It is not the act of witness that is primary; it is the act of faith, *to which* we witness, that is essential:

> It is to be considered, too, that to do the part of a witness for the truth, to warn and rebuke, is not an elementary duty of a Christian. I mean, that our duties come in a certain order, some before others, and that this is not one of the first of them. Our first duties are to repent and believe. It would be strange, indeed, for a man, who had just begun to think of religion, to set up for 'some great one', to assume he was a saint and a witness, and to exhort others to turn to God.[51]

To Newman this is an evident proposition; the living faith itself is the primary facet of Christian existence. It is only when this faith is truly alive that it can be witnessed to; without it, we are 'a noisy gong or a clanging cymbal'.[52]

48. *Ibid.*, p. 154.
49. *Ibid.*, p. 155.
50. *Ibid.*
51. *Ibid.*, p. 160.
52. 1 Cor 13:1.

When the faith is truly strong and alive, it can be witnessed to:

> But as time goes on, and his religious character becomes formed,
> then, while he goes on to perfection in all his duties, he takes
> upon himself, in the number of these, to witness for God by
> word of mouth.[53]

Such a task, when faith has become mature, is not just one choice
among others for the individual; for the Church is 'duty bound to
make a bold profession'.[54] The community as a whole is so bound;
it may sometimes occur, that an individual, by reason of his place
in life, is not called to such an act himself. Some are placed in these
posts, others are not; and these offices should not be intruded
upon.[55]

Once again Newman draws a line about church authority in
its teaching function: it lives indeed from the witness of the whole
Church, but, on its side, determines this witness. Despite per-
versions of this unity of balance, despite its being forgotten or
neglected: Newman's fundamental thought always reappears:
'Our light shall never go down; Christ set it upon a hill, and hell
shall not prevail against it. The Church will witness on to the last
for the truth.'[56] And this witness is its teaching.

As we saw, in 1830 Newman's activity as a public tutor at Oriel
College came to an end. His reaction to being relieved of these
duties was immediate: 'The Fathers arise again full before me', he
wrote, and his thoughts turned once more to his great project of
reading the Fathers through. He began to devote himself almost
exclusively to their study, and from this came his first great work,
The Arians of the Fourth Century.

53. *Ibid.*, pp. 160–61.
54. *Ibid.*, p. 162.
55. *Ibid.*, p. 163.
56. *Ibid.*, p. 164.

2

First Confrontation

In reply to a request from H. J. Rose, that he take part in a planned ecclesiastical history project, Newman answered that such a project would demand more work and time than he might be able to devote to such a comprehensive subject within the allotted span of time; otherwise he could see his way free for such an undertaking.[1] He had written earlier to another friend on the same subject, complaining that one had to write to please the 'dispatch of booksellers, who must sacrifice everything to regularity of publications and trimness of appearance'.[2] Newman felt that such a treatment left little room for the quality of research which such a subject ought to display; a church history, for example, should 'be derived from the original sources, and not be compiled from the standard authorities'. Years later he added a comment to the foot of this letter: 'My "Arians" was the result of this application.'[3] It was indeed.

Applying himself to the study of the Fathers for most of 1831, Newman found himself hard at work on an attempted history of the Councils; he never, however, got further than the introduction. It swelled and swelled under his hand, so much so, that Froude finally wrote him at the beginning of 1832 to 'stop fiddling with his introduction'.[4] But there seemed to be no end of difficulties; he wrote to Froude, just a few months before: 'My work opens a grand and most interesting field to me; but how I shall ever be able to make one assertion, much less to write one page, I cannot tell.'[5] In December of 1831 he is still dragging his feet; he mentions in his notes: 'resumed opusculum after many weeks' interruption.'

1. See *Letters* I, p. 210.
2. *Ibid.*, p. 207.
3. *Ibid.*
4. *Ibid.*, p. 223.
5. *Ibid.*, p. 216.

A later comment explains: 'I was working too hard at "The Arians". It was due the next summer, and I had only begun to read for it, or scarcely so, the summer past.'[6] But he did finish it on time, in July of 1832, noting, however, in his diary that 'the last days of my working upon the "Arians" I was tired wonderfully, continually on the point of fainting away, quite worn out'.[7] Upon completion, Newman was invited by Froude to take part in his planned voyage around the Mediterranean in hopes of bettering his already advanced tubercular condition. They set out in December of 1832, Newman having left his book in the hands of the printers. The state of overwork he was in during the final phases of *Arians* is evident in the obvious relief he experienced by the voyage, which lasted a good half a year.[8]

This volume, brought forth under such strain, deserves close attention. Though Newman's first major work and hence not so highly polished as later ones,[9] it presents major themes of his thought, themes which will be taken up again and again in his later writings. There is his oft repeated thought of the Church as always living;[10] there is his foretaste of Catholic principles;[11] more pertinent to our study, there is his conviction that the laity are fully qualified witnesses to the Catholic faith.[12] Inherent, too, in this work, described by some as being his first theological work and at the same time his most enduring,[13] are the balance points we have learned to look for in Newman's ruminations on the teaching function of the Church; he himself saw them more clearly later on and drew them out to their conclusions in the appendix he wrote for the third edition of *Arians* in 1871. Here, in 1832, we have the basis for his determination of 1871, his contention that the Church is dependent upon, and looks for, the witness of

6. *Ibid.*, p. 223.
7. *Ibid.*, p. 230.
8. See M. Ward, *Young Mr. Newman*, p. 191, where she describes him as being 'like steam expanding itself'.
9. Henry Wilberforce told him that, as far as he could judge, the style was not equal to that of his sermons; see *Letters* I, p. 230.
10. See L. Bouyer, *Newman, his Life and Spirituality*, p. 162.
11. Blanco White, the Spanish ex-priest who studied for a time with Newman at Oxford, wrote to Hawkins, the provost, that 'the whole of what Newman has worked out for his last publication—*Arians*—has been quite familiar to me since my youth'; see M. Ward, *Young Mr. Newman*, p. 144.
12. See M. Laros, 'Laie und Lehramt in der Kirche' in *Hochland* 37 (1939/40) 49.
13. See R. Greenfield, *The Attitude of the Tractarians to the Roman Catholic Church*, pp. 88–9.

the body of believers; that, however, the *ecclesia docens* determines the extent of this witness; and, finally, that the content of this witness of the faithful was given to them by the teaching authority of the Church.[14]

At the moment, however, and seen from his place in the Anglican Church, Newman was concerned with another problem. Beginning with the same fact, he was arriving at conclusions which were accented somewhat differently. He and his companions— Perceval and Froude—'were all becoming conscious of the importance of primitive tradition, and the Church as the tradition-bearing body'.[15] This, taking place as it did on the eve of the so-called Oxford Movement, was to have great effect later on, as we shall see. But, for the moment, we shall concentrate upon this thread of thought in itself, and try to trace it from its genesis to its completion, as far as Newman's treatment of it in *Arians* will allow.

Newman set out to write 'the history of Arianism';[16] as seen by him this would necessitate, for all practical purposes, a history of the Councils of the fourth century.[17] Expressed in the language of this study, he wanted to investigate the rise and fall of Arianism as a living idea within the pale of Christendom, as seen reflected in the actual witness of the Church: it's conciliar activity. In line with this thought, Newman sets the beginning of the heresy, the very root of it, in Antioch where, due to a myriad of pressures, the faith in Christ was becoming weaker and more anemic as the decades of the third century wore their way to a close.[18] The result: heresy. And it was strong. Newman describes its remarkable growth:

> In the course of six years it called for the interposition of a General Council; though of three hundred and eighteen bishops there assembled, only twenty-two, on the largest calculation and, as it really appears, only thirteen, were after all found to be its supporters. Though thus condemned by the whole Christian world, in a few years it broke out again; secured the patronage of the imperial court, which had recently been converted to the

14. See H. F. Davis, 'Le rôle et l'apostolat de la hiérarchie du laicat dans la théologie de l'Eglise chez Newman', p. 341; see also *Arians*, pp. 445–6.
15. Greenfield, *ibid.*, p. 96.
16. *Arians*, p. 1.
17. *Ibid.*, p 2.
18. *Ibid.*, p. 19.

Christian faith; made its way into the highest dignities of the Church; presided at her Councils, and tyrannized over the majority of her members who were orthodox believers.[19]

This growth, powerful enough in itself as it was, fed upon another factor which Newman noticed—the lack of an authoritative witness upon which the Church, as a whole, might fall back:

> . . . the absence of an adequate symbol of doctrine increased the evils thus existing, by affording an excuse and sometimes a reason for investigations, the necessity of which had not yet been superseded by the authority of an ecclesiastical decision. The traditionary system, received from the first age of the Church, had been as yet but partially set forth in authoritative forms; and by the time of the Nicene Council, the voices of the Apostles were but faintly heard throughout Christendom, and might be plausibly disregarded by those who were unwilling to hear.[20]

Here is the very seed of Newman's thought, as released by his study of the Arian heresy. 'The progress of unbelief naturally led them on to disparage, rather than to appeal to their predecessors; and to trust their cause to their own ingenuity . . .'[21] As faith cooled and became less conscious of its duties, the witness to that faith waned accordingly, and thus the traditions witnessed to by the Church became increasingly difficult to hear. The balance between the authority of the teaching Church and the regulative role of the witnessing Church was wrenched askew. This resulted in 'teaching them to regard the ecclesiastical authorities of former times as on a level with the uneducated and unenlightened of their own days'.[22]

With the balance necessary for the harmonious maintenance of the teaching function of the Church gone awry, it was necessary to take active steps for its return. This was not an easy task. The problem was, that, 'while the line of tradition, drawn out as it was to the distance of two centuries from the Apostles, had at length become of too frail a texture, to resist the touch of subtle and ill-directed reason', yet 'the Church was naturally unwilling to have

19. *Ibid.*, p. 25.
20. *Ibid.*, p. 35.
21. *Ibid.*, pp. 35–6.
22. *Ibid.*, p. 36.

recourse to the novel, though necessary measure, of imposing an authoritative creed upon those whom it invested with the office of teaching'.[23] Why this hesitancy? Newman felt that 'freedom from symbols and articles is abstractedly the highest state of Christian communion, and the peculiar privilege of the primitive Church';[24] and this for a variety of reasons. The basic foundation for this view was his admiration for the very balance between the authoritative and witnessing sides of the believing Church: the absence of creeds only makes this state more readily apparent and provides for its continuance. But up to a point, only: this Newman saw in the Arian controversy. And so he, as well as the prelates of the late third and early fourth centuries, 'were loth to confess, that the Church had grown too old to enjoy the free, unsuspicious teaching with which her childhood was blest; and that her disciples must, for the future, calculate and reason before they spoke and acted'.[25] They must calculate and reason in their role of ascertaining just *what* is the object of the Church's witness to its tradition.

The question was: where was the Church to take its source of witness? One might be tempted to answer: from Scripture. But, for Newman, this was an all-too simplistic answer. He calls it a 'general truth' that the doctrines of the Church 'have never been learned merely from Scripture'.[26] The Bible is, for Newman, a treacherous path to tread unguided, and the guidance needed for ascertaining the truth as revealed by God is to be found in the Church:

> Surely the Sacred Volume was never intended, and is not adapted, to teach us our creed; however certain it is that we can prove our creed from it, when it has once been taught us, and in spite of individual producible exceptions to the general rule. From the very first, that rule has been, as a matter of fact, that the Church should teach the truth, and then should appeal to Scripture in vindication of its own teaching.[27]

It is precisely here that the heretic makes his mistake. He neglects the source of truth provided for him and attempts a work which he cannot hope to accomplish: 'eliciting a systematic doctrine from the scattered notices of the truth which Scripture contains'.[28]

23. *Ibid.*
24. *Ibid.*
25. *Ibid.*, p. 37.

26. *Ibid.*, p. 50.
27. *Ibid.*
28. *Ibid.*

The insufficiency of Scripture by itself to lead through private study to all the truth it contains is shown by the fact that creeds and teachers have always been provided for its interpretation. It follows from this that:

> while inquirers and neophytes in the first centuries lawfully used the inspired writings for the purposes of morals and for instruction in the rudiments of the faith, they still might need the teaching of the Church as a key to the collection of passages which related to the mysteries of the Gospel, passages which are obscure from the necessity of combining and receiving them all.[29]

Thus the relation of Scripture to the tradition-bearing Church is analogous to that of the teaching authority within that Church to the whole Church. Just as the Scriptures bear witness to the revealed truth and the Church, bearing tradition as its marker, determines and manifests that witness, so also does the whole Church bear witness to that tradition which is determined in its extent by the teaching authority of the Church. Even in the primitive Church, still without the concretization of creeds, 'the truths reserved for the baptized Christian were not put forward as the arbitrary determinations of individuals, as the word of man, but rather as an apostolical legacy, preserved and dispensed by the Church'.[30]

But Scripture, as that original and primitive and divine witness to revealed truth, does not suffer under such a relationship; quite the contrary:

> . . . it must not be supposed, that this appeal to Tradition in the slightest degree disparages the sovereign authority and sufficiency of Holy Scripture, as a record of the truth . . . Apostolical Tradition is . . . not to supersede Scripture, but in conjunction with Scripture, to refute the self-authorized, arbitrary doctrines of heretics. We must cautiously distinguish . . . between a tradition supplanting or perverting the inspired records, and a corroborating, illustrating, and altogether subordinate tradition.[31]

Tradition, then, the authority which determines Scripture in its extent and which presents it to the whole Church as a record of the

29. *Ibid.*, p. 51.
30. *Ibid.*, p. 54.
31. *Ibid.*, p. 55.

original revelation, remains, despite its authority, *subordinate* to Scripture; it remains, in turn, itself determined by that original witness to the truth. Though tradition is here, and always will be, for Newman a guiding principle (especially in the form it took with primitive Christianity),[32] it is always under control from the very source over which it is to have authority. Not only the teaching function of the Church as practiced by the primitive Church is the essential norm for Newman, but also the original witness itself: the word of God.[33]

According to Biemer[34] Newman's problem did not consist in the insufficiency of Scripture, but in the insufficiency of its authorized interpreter. Thus tradition became for him an authorized exegete:

> The problem is not that of the 'existence and authority' of tradition, even of an apostolic tradition; much more it is the problem of verifying its authenticity and finding the means of guarding it from corruption.[35]

With this position Newman put himself in line with Palmer, Keble and the other high churchmen of the time:

> Unlike the Protestants, they did not believe in *sola scriptura*; unlike the Roman Catholics, they did not put tradition on an equal footing with the Bible. Having now come to this position, Newman went on to stress the importance of the tradition-bearing body, the Church.[36]

It is to this body that we now turn. Newman recognized what he called the 'divinity of Traditionary Religion'.[37] By this he meant that God had always spoken to man, that these utterances of God to man have been transported down through the ages, from man to man, from family to family; and that 'Revelation, properly speaking, is an universal, not a local gift'.[38] What, then, can possibly distinguish the Christian Church from any other religion? It is the

32. See G. Biemer, *Die Lehre von der Tradition nach J. H. Newman*, p. 93.
33. *Ibid.*, p. 95.
34. *Ibid.*, p. 99.
35. *Ibid.*, p. 98.
36. R. Greenfield, *The Attitude of the Tractarians to the Roman Catholic Church*, pp. 90–91.
37. *Arians*, p. 79.
38. *Ibid.*, p. 80.

fact that 'the Church of God ever has had, and the rest of mankind
never have had, authoritative documents of truth, and appointed
channels of communication with Him'.[39]

These documents—the Scriptures—are 'alone the depositary of
God's unadulterated and complete revelation'.[40] Yet, as complete
as this revelation as contained in Scripture is, it would be 'scarcely
more than a sealed book, needing an interpretation',[41] if it were
not for the Church, bearing in its tradition the principle necessary
for this interpretation. From the beginning the witness given by
revelation as found in Scripture was explained and determined
by the authority which taught within the Church. When, as in the
case of the Arian uproar, the balance, so carefully achieved, between
authority and witness is disrupted, the Church is 'bound to erect a
witness for the truth, which might be a guide and a warning to
all Catholics'.[42] That is, the teaching authority, basing itself on
the witness of the whole Church in its living faith, and determined
by this witness in its action, lays down as authentic and firm an
authoritative expression of this witness for the faith of the Church.
The Church must, says Newman, do so, in order to exclude error.[43]
And we exclude error in order to secure the community of faith
in its belief.

Scripture, says Newman, is not 'sufficient for the purposes of
Christian fellowship'.[44] It is tradition, as proposed by the teaching
Church in its role as expounder of Scripture, which gives the final
word to preserving the faith of the community:

> Scripture being unsystematic, and the faith which it propounds
> being scattered through its documents, and understood only
> when they are viewed as a whole, the Creeds aim at concentrating
> its general spirit, so as to give security to the Church, as far as
> may be, that its members take that definite view of that faith
> which alone is the true one.[45]

This is definitely an office of the Church: it is one of the basic duties
of the Christian to inculcate that character of faith and witness

39. *Ibid.*
40. *Ibid.*, pp. 83–4.
41. *Ibid.*, p. 135.
42. *Ibid.*, p. 143.
43. *Ibid.*, p. 146.
44. *Ibid.*
45. *Ibid.*, p. 147.

which is necessary for the maintenance of the Church as a community of believers.

Newman sums up his thought on this office of the Church in one of those passages which ring with the beauty of his language:

> If the Church be the pillar and ground of truth, and bound to contend for the preservation of the faith once delivered to it; if we are answerable as ministers of Christ for the formation of one, and one only, character in the heart of man; and if Scriptures are given us, as a means indeed towards that end, but inadequate to the office of interpreting themselves, except to such as live under the same Divine Influence which inspired them, and which is expressly sent down upon us that we may interpret them— then, it is evidently our duty piously and cautiously to collect the sense of Scripture, and solemnly to promulgate it in such a form as is best suited, as far as it goes, to exclude the pride and unbelief of the world.[46]

There are several important points in this passage which are vital to his conception of the teaching function of the Church:

1) Newman sees the Church as the 'pillar and ground of truth', one of his favorite phrases in describing the Church in its mission. The Church exists in order to preserve and carry on the truth of Christ's revelation of God; it is to preserve this truth unsullied and until the end of time. It is the bearer of this truth, and the only bearer. This is the main task of the Church, and should overshadow all others: the Church is *the* witness to the revelation of Christ and its most important duty is to manifest that revealed truth to the world through its constant witness thereto.

2) The ministers of this Church are the means by which the Church fulfills that mission. They are answerable to the Church and thus to Christ; in other words, they are answerable to the very truth to which they are to bear witness. To bear a true witness to the truth of revelation is to be true to Christ. The guiding principle for any minister—and hence for the teaching authority in the Church—is to be true to the witness of the Church to its faith. Manifesting that witness to the world and to the Church is the essential function of the Church's ministers.

3) Scripture, the font and original witness to the revealed truth of Christ, is not, in itself, able to fully manifest its witness. It must

46. *Ibid.*, p. 148.

be expounded and witnessed to by tradition—thus evidencing that same relationship which exists between the witnessing Church and its teaching authority.

4) This all, however, says Newman in a last point, is a discharge of office which 'is the most momentous and fearful that can come upon mortal man, and never to be undertaken except by the collective illumination of the Heads of the Church . . .'.[47] In other words, it is as obedient to the witness and faith of the *whole* Church that the ministers of the teaching Church are to fulfill their function. And they are to undertake this office of theirs together, exemplifying the unity of the Church in their actions.[48]

Newman, having worked out the principles governing the teaching function of the Church in light of his investigations into the Arian heresy, now goes directly to the history of that movement in order to see if that is what really happened. He finds the settlement of it, the ironing out of the doctrine concerning the divinity of Christ, reaching its high point in the acceptance, at the Council of Nicaea, of the *homoousian* formula expressing our Lord's relationship to the Father. It was accepted, says Newman, 'as a symbol, for securing the doctrine of our Lord's divinity, first by the infallible authority of the Nicene Council, and next by the experimental assent and consent of Christendom'.[49]

Those notes of the teaching Church, as outlined above, are plain to see in this instance: the Church's teaching authority only entered upon its task when the security of the faith demanded it; and then only in conjunction with the whole Church. First, the assembled ministers of the teaching Church, in council, proclaim a definitive witness to the truth of revelation; but then the *whole* Church—Christendom—actively accepts this witness to the faith as true and assents in it.

This should not be misinterpreted as an attempt to caste the

47. *Ibid.*, p. 149.
48. See *Lumen Gentium* of Vatican II, §22: *Ordo autem Episcoporum, qui collegio Apostolorum in magisterio et regimine pastorali succedit, immo in quo corpus apostolicum continuo perseverat . . . subiectum quoque supremae ac plena potestatis in universam Ecclesiam existit . . .* ; and §25: *Episcopi in communione cum Romano Pontifice docentes ab omnibus tamquam divinae et catholicae veritatis testes venerandi sunt . . .* Though Newman had just written his first book, at the age of thirty-one, and was still deeply committed to the Church of England, the similarity between his views as outlined above, and those of the Second Vatican Council, more than 130 years later, is striking.
49. *Ath. Trans.* II, p. 438.

Church's teaching function as a parliamentary agreement, but rather must be seen in light of Newman's thought as given above: these two actions—the definitive decision by the teaching authority and the assent of Christendom—are an organic unity and their being differentiated in time is only secondary. In time, the order could just as well be reversed; in fact, it normally is. But the principle remains firm as regards the Church as a whole: 'The Ecclesiastical Body is a divinely-appointed means, towards realizing the great evangelical blessings.'[50]

It is the whole Church, the universal Church, which is the ultimate base upon which the teaching ministration within that Church can operate.[51] This can be seen even more clearly in the actual role played by the witnessing part of the Church, the people reacting in their faith. It was a time which demanded the most from the Church, a time filled with disasters. But let Newman tell it:

> At this critical moment Constantius died, when the cause of truth was only not in the lowest state of degradation, because a party was in authority and vigour who could reduce it to a lower still; the Latins committed to an Anti-Catholic Creed, the Pope deluded, Hosius fallen and dead; Athanasius wandering in the deserts, Arians in the sees of Christendom, and their doctrine growing in blasphemy, and their profession of it in boldness, every day. The Emperor had come to the throne almost when a boy, and at this time was but forty-four years old. In the ordinary course of things he might have reigned till, humanly speaking, orthodoxy was extinct.[52]

At this point the ruling civilian powers made a fatal mistake. They assumed that 'whatever shows itself on the surface of the Apostolic Community, its prominences and irregularities, all that is extravagant, and all that is transitory, is the real moving principle and life of the system'.[53] But that was not the case. The Church was not to stand and fall on the witness of a few; rather it was 'the thousands of silent believers, who worshipped in spirit and in truth, who were obscured by the tens and twenties of the various heretical factions'.[54]

50. *Arians,* p. 258.
51. *Ibid.,* p. 265.
52. *Ath. Trans.* I, pp. 121–2: n.b. 1.
53. *Arians,* pp. 354–5.
54. *Ibid.*

Speaking of Athanasius, Newman makes this clearer. For Athanasius the 'voice of the Christian people' was one of the mainstays of the Church's doctrine. He himself, remaining true to this voice, was 'in no sense an inquirer, nor a mere disputant; he has received, and he transmits'.[55] That this voice of the people could be so important to Athanasius, that great Father of the Church during the fourth century, is only in line with what Newman has been saying up to now. But he goes further and cites Hilary of Poitiers, who remarked upon the laity under the pressure of the Arian heresy: 'The ears of the people are holier than the hearts of the priests.'[56] Newman felt that these remarks could be applied to many of the bishops of that period who had arianized.[57] For it was the faithful who remained firm and gave witness to the true faith, and it was upon that witness that the teaching authority of the Church built its defense of the faith.

Even at this early stage in his thought Newman was convinced, and the more so because of his historical investigations, that the Church was only able to fulfill its duty of teaching the faith, true and pure, when based upon a balance of the authority and the witness given within the whole Church. And only upon such a balance.

Upon finishing his study of the Arian heresy, Newman made ready to depart on his journey with his friend Froude around the Mediterranean. But he did so foreseeing what lay ahead for him and the Church of England:

And so of the present perils, with which our branch of the Church is beset, as they bear a marked resemblance to those of the fourth century, so are the lessons, which we gain from that ancient time, especially cheering and edifying to Christians of the present day. Then as now, there was the prospect, and partly the presence in the Church, of an Heretical Power enthralling it, exerting a varied influence and a usurped claim in the appointment of her functionaries, and interfering with the management of her internal affairs.[58]

---

55. *Ath. Trans.* II, p. 250.
56. *Sanctiores sunt aures plebis, quam corda sacerdotum*; see *Arians*, p. 358.
57. *Ibid.*; in the 3rd edition (1871) Newman at this point refers the reader to the appendix—dealing with the subject of the laity's witness to the faith—which he had composed from his famous article in the *Rambler* on the same topic in 1859; he obviously felt that the words of Hilary could be brought in defense of his own views on the subject. See below, chapter 11.
58. *Ibid.*, p. 393.

But they could hope and have confidence in the Lord that 'should the hand of Satan press us sore, our Athanasius, and Basil will be given us in their destined season, to break the bonds of the Oppressor, and let the captives go free'.[59] Thus, before the year 1832 was out, Newman foretold the rising of that movement in the Church of England called after his university: the Oxford Movement.

59. *Ibid.*, p. 394.

3

The Oxford Movement: a Via Media

In speaking of the Church, I mean of course the laity, as well as the clergy in their three orders—the whole body of Christians united, according to the will of Jesus Christ, under the Successors of the Apostles.[1]

—John Keble

In these words, from the famous sermon which for Newman figured as the beginning of the Oxford Movement,[2] we find the basic ideas of the Tractarians. Newman had returned to Oxford from Sicily on the very day that Keble preached his sermon and saw in it a call to battle for the principles it enunciated.

Some of the most prominent figures in the Movement—Froude, Palmer, Perceval—met at Hadleigh from 25 to 29 July to plan a course of action. There they came up with two ideas: an association for the defense of the Church and a series of tracts to publicize their efforts.[3] Nothing came of these plans until Newman decided to take a course of action himself; writing in his diary, he records in a characteristically brief sentence his first step: 'I thought I brought out the first Tract in the course of August, but the printer's bill dates it September 9.'[4] Dean Church, composer of the finest account of that Movement, sees it in a different, and for our purposes, more important light:

> . . . it was not till Mr. Newman made up his mind to force on the public mind, in a way which could not be evaded, the great article of the Creed—'I believe one Catholic and Apostolic Church'—that the movement began.[5]

1. *National Apostasy: considered in a sermon preached in St. Mary's, Oxford, before the Judges of Assize, Sunday, July 14, 1833*, Oxford, 1833.
2. See *Letters* I, p. 379.
3. *Ibid.*, pp. 379–80.
4. *Ibid.*, p. 381.
5. Dean Church, *The Oxford Movement*, London, 3rd edition, 1922, p. 33.

In other words, Newman saw something in Keble's sermon which fitted the situation in England as we saw him describe it at the end of *Arians*. What had been a squabble, however, over ten superfluous bishoprics in Ireland about to be suppressed, was turned by Newman into an action to reform the Church.[6] The original problem—whether the state, in the form of legislation, could have power over the existence or non-existence of bishops and dioceses—soon grew into something far more important and far more extensive than even Keble might have imagined as he wrote the words to his sermon on apostasy.

Newman, in the meantime, was hard at work. Towards the end of 1833 he began 'reprinting his tracts most earnestly, and distributing them'.[7] The Movement was in full swing, and it began to center itself around the question of church authority and in what form such authority manifested itself. In Keble's words, already cited,[8] the authority of the Church consisted in the whole of the community, under the guidance of its bishops. Newman took this basic thought, already familiar to him from the studies involved in his composition of *Arians*, and began to build. Such thought, of course, was basic to them all, for Bishop Lloyd of Oxford and a divinity professor at Oxford in the years preceding the Movement, used to gather those who would later be its leaders into seminars where 'he taught his pupils the doctrines of Church Authority, Apostolic Succession, and Episcopacy which were to find their way into many of the Tracts'.[9]

It is this thought on the authority of the Church, especially as it touches the teaching function of the Church, which we will now follow in its initial stages in the Oxford Movement. We will see later how the seeds planted here led to Newman's overbalancing of the role of ecclesiastical authority in teaching and paved the way for his journey to Rome.

'With the confidence of one under authority Newman proclaimed the faith of the universal Church . . .'[10] Filled with a sense of mission, Newman took upon himself the major task of announcing anew those doctrines he held for essential to the Church, but which had been forgotten. 'Keble had given the inspiration', says

6. *V.M.* II, p. 23.
7. *Letters* I, p. 381.
8. See above, footnote 1.
9. R. Greenfield, *The Attitude of the Tractarians to the Roman Catholic Church,* p. 8.
10. O. Chadwick, *The Victorian Church* I, p. 197.

Dean Church, 'Froude had given the impulse; then Newman took up the work, and the impulse henceforward, and the direction, were his.'[11] To its direction Newman brought his own concerns of the role authority had to play in a Christian community. Long convinced of the necessary role for received and binding teachings in religion, as we have seen, he now saw the same problematic stretched out on a national scale: 'The Oxford Movement was to be a last desperate struggle to keep in the Church of England the dogmatic principle.'[12]

This concern did not forget the basic task of Christianity, the holiness and salvation of souls; on the contrary, men were impressed from the first, men who did not agree conceptually with the Tractarians, by the degree of personal holiness evinced in them and their constant call to such a state. In fact, these two concerns were intimately related:

> ... there was no contradiction in Newman's thought ... between the deep spiritual aims of the Movement and its insistence on such matters as Apostolic Succession . . . Only a religion of authority could ever be for the mass of men a religion of the spirit, could save men's souls from the world and the devil and make them ready to stand before God.[13]

But Newman was not simply banking upon the authority present in the Church to perform the necessary task at hand; his view, always striving towards a balance, could not but take up the missing side. In a letter home from Rome during his trip in 1833, we find him saying:

> If we look into history, whether in the age of the Apostles, St. Ambrose's or St. Beckett's, still the people were the fulcrum of the Church's power. So they may be again.[14]

The fulcrum, he said. If our analysis of the role played by the *whole* Church up to now has been valid, then Newman is here simply reiterating his stand that the witnessing action of the *whole* Church gives the power—i.e. the authority—in the Church its basis for action. For Newman, in accentuating what Chadwick calls the key

11. Church, *The Oxford Movement*, p. 32.
12. Ward, *Young Mr. Newman*, p. 92.
13. *Ibid.*, p. 237.
14. As quoted in Ward, *Young Mr. Newman*, p. 224.

principles of the Oxford Movement—'the idea of apostolic succession and its connexion with the independent authority of the
Church'[15]—was concerned with *how* the Church might survive
on its *own* authority without the support of the state. To solve this
problem, he needed to delineate the foundations of that power;
and in doing this, he was forced to investigate the role of this power
in the teaching activity of the Church.

At this time, shortly after his return from the Mediterranean,
Newman composed an article which was intended to be the first
in a series entitled 'Home Thoughts Abroad'; but as this series was
never continued, it remained the sole example.[16] It was not
published until three years later, 1836, in the *British Magazine*.
When Newman republished it in his *Discussions and Arguments* in
1872 he retitled it 'How to Accomplish it'—a title, incidentally,
indicative of how the early Tractarians thought of their undertaking.[17] This short sketch, in the form of a dialogue,[18] aims, in
Newman's explanatory words, at 'giving vitality' to the English
Church; one protagonist—the role taken by Froude—sees this in
union with Rome; the narrator—Newman—sees it as best accom-
plished in developing a nineteenth-century Anglo-Catholicism.[19]
It deals mainly, but in an early stage of development, with the
Anglican theory of the *via media* and thus illustrates the fact that
Newman, even at this early date, 1833, was aware of and wrestling
with the problem of the churches, or, how could there be authority
in a divided Church?[20]

The discussion is opened with a reflection upon recent events in

15. Chadwick, *The Victorian Church* I, p. 71.
16. *Dis. Arg.,* p. v.
17. In R. Greenfield, *The Tractarians and the Roman Catholic Church,* p. 146,
there is an account of how H. Rose, at that time editor of the *British Magazine*,
shelved the article due to its romanizing overtones; Newman was thus able to
publish it at last when he himself became editor of the same publication. That he
truly had written it at such an early date is evidenced by a letter he wrote to
Froude on 2 September 1833 (*Letters* I, p. 397) in which Newman mentions
something he had written and the consequent criticism of it by Froude; there
is a note added at some later date identifying the object of Froude's words as
'Home Thoughts'.
18. Ward (*Young Mr. Newman*, p. 206) follows Christopher Dawson in identifying the participants in the conversation as Ambrose = Hurrell Froude and
Cyril = Newman himself.
19. *Dis. Arg.,* p. 1.
20. See J. Stern, 'Traditions apostoliques et Magistère selon J. H. Newman' in
Revue des sciences philosophiques et théologiques 47 (1963) 36.

England, 'which had saddened us both, as leading us to forebode
the overthrow of all that gives dignity and interest to our country'.[21]
As regards the Church, they expect evil[22] and find it impossible
to believe that it 'depends for its existence on what is without, so as
to be dissipated and to vanish at once upon the occurrence of certain
changes in public affairs'.[23]

The concern here is for the independent authority of the Church,
but it is not enough simply to maintain it: they must establish it.
But 'there is such a religious *fact* as the existence of a great Catholic
body, union with which is a Christian privilege and duty. Now,
we English are separate from it.'[24] By this is meant the Roman
communion, which, though in the eyes of the Anglicans not the
whole Church, formed an essential branch of the divided whole of
Christendom. This division was tolerated on the principle of truth:
'The Church is founded on a doctrine—the gospel of *Truth*.'[25]

This is an expression of the famous 'branch theory' of Anglican
ecclesiology which found expression in the *via media* developed by
the Tractarians. This branch theory, as posed by them, had but
one task: 'Anglican ecclesiology is characterized by its relationship
to the branch churches . . . its essential function is to maintain the
genuine Word of God in an incorrupt condition and to pass it on
without misuse or addition . . . but it is nothing more than this.'[26]
As an expression of the divisions found in Christianity, however, its
function was limited to pointing out the basic unity of the Church
catholic as embodied in the fact that all the various divisions in the
Church do not exist in themselves but only insofar as they still
partake in the one power and unity of the whole Church:

> In this Church there can be no division. Pass the axe through it,
> and one part or the other is cut off from the Apostles. There
> cannot be two distinct bodies, each claiming descent from the
> original stem. Indeed, the very word *catholic* witnesses to this.
> Two Apostolic bodies there may be without actual contradiction
> of terms; but there is necessarily but one body Catholic.[27]

21. *Dis. Arg.*, p. 3.
22. *Ibid.*
23. *Ibid.*, p. 4.
24. *Ibid.*, p. 5.
25. *Ibid.*
26. G. Biemer, *Die Lehre von der Tradition nach J. H. Newman*, p. 48.
27. *Dis. Arg.*, p. 6.

The problem is to base the authority of the present-day Church upon that of the primitive, undivided apostolic Church catholic.

One cannot indiscriminately apply the words and standards of the Church of the Fathers to the present-day churches. 'The tradition of the early Church was of an historical character, of the nature of testimony; and possessed an authority superadded to the Church's proper authority as a divine institution.'[28] It was historical because it witnessed to facts of the apostolic era, but it did not equal the authority inherent in the Church as a divine institution.

Here Newman is reacting to an exaggerated view of the power of traditionary witness. The witness of the whole Church achieves its validity in its determination and guidance through the authorities given the Church in the name of the Apostles. Thus, says Newman, such witness in itself was 'virtually infallible. Now, however, this accidental authority has long ceased . . .'.[29] That is, we cannot use it any longer to provide an answer to the lack of unity in Christianity as regards the question of authority. The only possible and viable way of action is the branch theory.

This can be countered, however, on the grounds that it is a 'theory which has never been realized'.[30] That one could avoid the Romanist position and yet not be ranked in the Protestant rolls, i.e. take a *via media* based upon a preservation of primitive and apostolic tradition,[31] simply has never been proven: 'The actual English Church has never adopted it: in spite of the learning of her divines, she has ranked herself among the Protestants, and the doctrine of the Via Media has slept in libraries.'[32]

What then is to be done? They must find the basis for authority in the Church which will allow the Church to subsist independent of any outside support. For 'if the State declares it has itself no divine right over us, what help is there for it? We must learn, like Hagar, to subsist by ourselves in the wilderness.'[33] This is so because, to come to the root of the problem, the Anglican Church (and, for that matter, any of the divided branches of Christianity) has 'no *church* basis':[34]

28. *Ibid.*, p. 11.
29. *Ibid.*
30. *Ibid.*, p. 17.
31. See above, footnote 26.
32. *Dis. Arg.*, p. 18.
33. *Ibid.*, p. 22.
34. *Ibid.*, p. 33.

The Church in England is not a body now, it has little or no substantiveness; it has dwindled down to its ministers, who are as much secular functionaries as they are rulers of a Christian people . . . the problem is, How to do it?[35]

It was in answer to this problem that Newman began the unfolding of his *via media*, an attempt to make it real and not just the relic of dusty book shelves. When this attempt proved impossible, then it was that Newman turned towards Rome and its exaggerated sense of authority.

His first clear statement of the *via media* found its place in tracts 38 and 41 of the *Tracts for the Times*.[36] He begins by pointing out that the present-day Anglicanism had changed from the position of the first reformers to one much nearer to Protestantism.[37] But this was not what had made the Anglican Church to be what it was for the first reformers:

The glory of the English Church is, that it has taken the VIA MEDIA, as it has been called. It lies *between* the (so called) Reformers and the Romanists.[38]

This position cannot 'consent . . . to deprive itself of the Church's dowry, the doctrines which the Apostles spoke in Scripture and impressed upon the early Church'.[39] Thus the Church takes the role of a 'messenger from Christ, rich in treasures old and new, rich with the accumulated wealth of ages'.[40] It brings 'monuments of Truth' which are records of the Church's witnessing to its faith; it is upon this witness, and not upon historical traditions, that the Church is to base its authority.

More than individual creeds or formulations of doctrines one is bound to believe the *whole* gospel; this takes its form, in a living, day-to-day expression, in the 'Liturgy, as coming down from the Apostles' and is thus, and precisely as living, 'the depository of their complete teaching'.[41] Thus the 'Christian minister should be a

---

35. *Ibid.*, p. 35.
36. Both written in 1834 and republished in *V.M.* II; Newman, however, mistakenly numbers the second one 40 instead of 41.
37. *V.M.* II, p. 26.
38. *Ibid.*, p. 28.
39. *Ibid.*, p. 31.
40. *Ibid.*
41. *Ibid.*, p. 33.

witness against the errors of his day',[42] and by implication, to the eternal truths of the gospel.

Would this really stand up to a rigorous comparison with primitive Christianity? Precisely this question—the search for a living *via media*—led to one of the first fruits of the Oxford Movement: the studies in primitive Christianity.[43]

42. *Ibid.*
43. *Apol.*, p. 73.

4

Primitive Christianity

When Newman wrote the papers entitled *Primitive Christianity* (1833–1836), the Oxford Movement was in its first stages. The papers are an attempt to link that effort with the primitive Christianity he felt to be so necessary for the foundation of the Church.[1] Republishing them in 1872 he states that 'They were written under the assumption that the Anglican Church has a place, as such, in Catholic communion and Apostolic Christianity.' But this is for him 'a question of fact, which the Author would now of course answer in the negative, retaining still, and claiming as his own, the positive principles and doctrines which that fact is, in these Papers taken to involve'.[2]

Thus we are more than justified to subject these early studies to a closer scrutiny, especially since they deal with our very topic. Newman begins by stating the situation in which the Anglican Church finds itself under the patronage of governmental support, then indicates that the gospel truth, as such, is not his interest here, for 'Truth, indeed, will always support itself in the world by its native vigour . . . this was the case before our Lord came.'[3] His subject is, however, of a much more subjective nature:

> My question concerns *the Church*, that peculiar institution which Christ set up as a visible home and memorial of Truth; and which,

1. See *Letters* I, p. 396, where Newman, in a letter to F. Rogers, notes the beginning of this work: 'I have been writing a series of papers for Rose, called the "Church of the Fathers", which commences in October . . .' The date: 31 August 1833. Almost six and a half years later he writes (*Letters* II, p. 267) to J. W. Bowden that 'my "Church of the Fathers" is now finished. It is the prettiest book I have done; which is not wonderful, being hardly more than the words and works of the Fathers.' This 'prettiest' book he had done is now to be found in his *Historical Sketches* I, pp. 333–446.
2. *Hist. Sketch*. I, p. 335.
3. *Ibid.,* p. 339.

as being in this world, must be manifested by means of this world.[4]

Here we have an early, and essential, description of the Church. Newman sees it as: 1) instituted by Christ; 2) as a 'home' or depository of Truth, whereby he means the truth of the Gospel, revelation; 3) and, most important, as a 'memorial of Truth'— that is, a teacher (The choice of the word 'memorial' is indicative of his conception of how this teaching is to function: not as a laying down of certain rules, concretized formulae, rigid, unbending and lifeless collections of words. It is much more a *witness,* a memorial to that truth given to the Church in living fashion by its founder. It is to this living truth that the Church is a memorial, a witness: witnessing to its life *and* living, but not—above all not—determining this truth as if it had formed it itself.); and 4) since it is in the world, its functions are manifested by 'means of this world'. That is, as human beings living within the world as we *know* it, so will we also function within the Church; for the eye of faith is not the eye of knowledge.[5] Thus the act of witnessing to the truth given it will be performed by the Church within the bounds and limits imposed by the possibilities for manifestation as set by the world we dwell within.

He goes on to describe how, up to that moment, the Church of England had functioned within its world: 'Hitherto the English Church has depended on the State, i.e. on the ruling powers in the country—the king and the aristocracy,'[6] and up to now this has not been an altogether unprofitable relationship:

This is so natural and religious a position of things when viewed in the abstract, and in its actual working has been productive of such excellent fruits in the Church, such quietness, such sobriety, such external propriety of conduct, and such freedom from doctrinal excesses, that we must ever look back upon the period of ecclesiastical history so characterized with affectionate thoughts.[7]

But this will do no longer; this power, as a ruling power of the Church, has ceased to be. Hence he asks himself: what is to take

4. *Ibid.,* pp. 339–40.
5. St. Thomas Aquinas, *Summa Theologiae,* II^a–II^{ae}, q. 4, a. 1.
6. *Hist. Sketch.* I, p. 340.
7. *Ibid.*

the place of this governmental support of the Church? The answer
is quick in coming, though hard on the palate:

> . . . these recollections of the past . . . must not hinder us from
> . . . inquiring what is intended by Providence to take the place of
> the timehonoured instrument, which He has broken (if it be yet
> broken), the regal and aristocratical power. I shall offend many
> men when I say, we must *look to the people*;[8] but let them give
> me a hearing.[9]

Let us not, however, be misled into thinking that Newman has here
approached a conception of the people of God as theologically and
functionally playing their proper role. He is still ambivalent and
uncertain; he himself, influenced by the university world of
Oxford, by his seat in a hierarchical world, still views 'the people'
in a dichotomy with the clergy:

> Who at first sight does not dislike the thoughts of gentlemen and
> clergy men depending for their maintenance and their reputation
> on their flocks? of their strength, as a visible power, lying not
> in their birth, the patronage of the great, and the endowment
> of the Church (as hitherto), but in the homage of a multitude?
> I confess I have before now had a great repugnance to the notion
> myself.[10]

Here we have an indication of how Newman's upbringing and
education influenced his thought at this early stage in his development. Himself a member, through Oxford, of the Establishment,
he had great reluctance in turning from it to 'the people', i.e. the
lower classes, the representatives, in the mind of the Establishment,
of all that was uncultured, uneducated and backward. It was no
great theological insight that brought Newman from his hope in
this Establishment to the people:

> . . . if I have overcome it [his repugnance], and turned from the
> Government to the People, it has been simply because I was
> forced to do so. It is not we who desert the Government, but

8. Ward (*Young Mr. Newman,* p. 224) cites a letter written from Rome in
1833 to 'a former pupil' where Newman strikes this very point: 'If we look into
history, whether in the age of the Apostles, St. Ambrose's or St. Beckett's, still
the people were the fulcrum of the Church's power. So they may be again.'
9. *Hist. Sketch.* I, p. 340.
10. *Ibid.,* p. 341.

the Government that has left us; we are forced back upon those below us, because those above us will not honour us; there is not help for it, I say.[11]

Thus, in Newman's mind, the government had given up its task to guard and guide the Church as it should; it had forfeited its claim to allegiance from the Church because derelict in its duties; it had failed, and miserably so, and thus must be severed from the Church.

For Newman there is no other way to turn but to the people. Echoing ever so slightly the *narodni* movement in Russia later in the century (though devoid of the latter's messianic overtones), he sees the Church's only hope for support resting in the people. Yet in truth it will not be so bad; basing himself on the apostolic succession, Newman finds the people as supporters of the Church no great essential danger:

> . . . in truth, the prospect is not so bad as it seems at first sight. The chief and obvious objection to the clergy being thrown on the People, lies in the probable lowering of Christian views, and the adulation of the vulgar, which would be its consequence; . . . But let us recollect that we are an apostolical body; we are not made, nor can be unmade by our flocks and if our influence is to depend on *them*, yet the Sacraments reside with *us*. We have that with us, which none but ourselves possess, the mantle of the Apostles; and this, properly understood and cherished, will ever keep us from being creatures of a populace.[12]

Here it is obvious that Newman still retains the traditional dichotomy of laity and clergy on the basis of a simplistic and superficial separation according to class and education. His thought is young and undeveloped; we must follow it through his later work to find its fuller unfolding and comprehension.[13]

In the studies which follow Newman is concerned with pointing out that 'the Church, when purest and when most powerful, *has*

11. *Ibid.*
12. *Ibid.*
13. He goes on in the same passage to point out that 'what may become necessary in time to come, is a more religious state of things also'. How? '. . . according to the Scripture view of the Church, though all are admitted into her pale, and the rich inclusively, yet, the poor are her members with a peculiar suitableness, and by a special right'—again, a distinction based upon a social position and quite illustrative of Newman's ambivalence.

depended for its influence on its consideration with the many'.[14]
He is thinking here primarily of the 'primitive Church—the
Church of St. Athanasius and St. Ambrose'. In our consideration
of his work *The Arians of the Fourth Century* we have seen him
handle this topic in regard to Athanasius; now the focus shifts to
Ambrose and the Western Church.

In his account of Ambrose's conflict with Valentinian for the
possession of a church in Milan by the Arians, Newman accentuates
the role played by the people. He recounts that when Ambrose
refused to surrender the church demanded by the government
officials for the Arian community in Milan, he had 'rested his
resistance on grounds which the people understood at once, and
recognized as irrefragable. They felt that he was only refusing to
surrender a trust. They rose in a body, and thronged the palace
gates'.[15] But Newman is at pains to show that Ambrose was not
a captive of his own church. It may well be true that it is the support
of the people which carries Ambrose to victory but Newman's
point is to show 'how a Church may be in "favour with all the
people" without any subserviency to them'.[16]

Ambrose is still the leader and teacher of his flock. Quoting
from his letters at the time, Newman illustrates this in the words of
the heroic bishop, who describes the siege in his basilica, during
which he restrains the crowd from violent action and seeks to
occupy them with other activities. Among these he introduces
hymns in praise of the Trinity, and comments on the charge that
the people were being misled by them:

> For can any strain have more of influence than the confession of
> the Holy Trinity, which is proclaimed day by day by the
> voice of the whole people? Each is eager to rival his fellows in
> confessing, as he well knows how, in sacred verses, his faith in
> Father, Son, and Holy Spirit. Thus all are made teachers, who
> else were scarce equal to being scholars.[17]

These words of Ambrose Newman makes his own in the development of his thought; for here we see the accent once more on the
witnessing function of teaching. All are teachers *insofar* as they

14. *Ibid.*, p. 342.
15. *Ibid.*, p. 347.
16. *Ibid.*, p. 348.
17. *Ibid.*, p. 356.

witness to the faith; in this case given them by their bishop, witnessed to by their bishop. For Ambrose, to witness to the faith is to teach it.

Newman takes up the thread of this thought in the discussion which follows of Vincent of Lerins. He begins his discussion by castigating the opinion of the Church's mission which maintains that 'the highest end of Church union, to which the mass of educated men now look, is quiet and unanimity'.[18] But this happy middle, which for Newman is just one more expression of the desire for comfort and a lessening of effort on the part of the Christianity of his day, is not the alpha and omega of the Church's purpose in this world; it postulates a standpoint which functions 'as if the Church were not built upon faith, and truth really the first object of the Christian's efforts, peace but the second'.[19]

Striving for peace is but one of many duties imposed upon the Christian; there are other duties too, and far more important ones at that. He continues: 'Now I make bold to say, that confessorship for the Catholic faith is one part of the duty of Christian ministers, nay, and Christian laymen too.'[20] Newman is here grappling with a major idea. He is attempting to express his belief, here in its first stages of development, that it is the whole Church, lay and clerical, which has the God-given duty of confessing, witnessing, to its trust: the faith. This is for him the most important task given the Church. Without the faith, what can remain? 'Surely the Church exists, in an especial way, for the sake of the faith committed to her keeping.'[21]

Granted this supposition, Newman then asks the question, where is this creed of faith to be found? Supposing the question is put, are Ambrose, Leo and Gregory right? Would these same Fathers of the Church have been right to raise the same question themselves?[22] He answers by asking a question in return: how do we know that the Fathers and we are right in receiving the epistles of Paul the Apostle?[23] He answers that it 'is a matter of history' that they are Paul's letters.[24] And what is meant by its being a matter of history?

18. *Ibid.*, p. 375.
19. *Ibid.*
20. *Ibid.*, p. 376.
21. *Ibid.*
22. *Ibid.*, p. 380.
23. *Ibid.*
24. *Ibid.*

Why, that it has ever been so believed, so declared, so recorded, so acted on, from the first down to this day; that there is no assignable point of time when it was not believed, no assignable point at which the belief was introduced; that the records of past ages fade away and vanish *in* the belief; that in proportion as past ages speak at all, they speak in one way, and only fail to bear a witness, when they fail to have a voice. What stronger testimony can we have of a past fact?[25]

This is tradition and for Newman there was no stronger testimony to a past fact: the Church having witnessed always and everywhere to a particular doctrine; that it has 'never and nowhere *not* been maintained'.[26] For Newman this is the great 'canon of the *Quod semper, quod ubique, quod ab omnibus,* which saves us from the misery of having to find out the truth for ourselves from Scripture on our independent and private judgment'.[27]

It is not by accident that this canon is present in the Church's conscience; in Newman's mind, 'He who gave Scripture, also gave us the interpretation of Scripture; and He gave the one and the other gift in the same way, by the testimony of past ages, as matter of historical knowledge, or as it is sometimes called, by Tradition.'[28]

Here Newman is denoting a doctrine common to the Anglican theological stream in which he lived.[29] He had come in contact

25. *Ibid.*
26. *Ibid.*
27. *Ibid.*, p. 381. At this stage in Newman's development this rule of thumb served him well and he found it to be a vital unit in his thought; later he was to give it up as being too weak by itself. The text Newman is recalling to mind here, and which he quotes later on in the article in translation, is the famous opening passage of Vincent of Lerins' *Commonitorium* I (PL 50) where Vincent speaks thus of tradition: *In ipsa item Catholica Ecclesia magnopere curandum est ut id teneamus quod ubique, quod semper, quod ab omnibus creditum est.* Later in the same work Vincent speaks of the *depositum* (cap. XXII, 667) and says it should be *publicae traditionis . . . in qua non auctor debes esse, sed custor.* This is, as we shall see, a typical thought of Newman's and indicates his debt to Vincent in the working out of his ideas on tradition.
28. *Ibid.*
29. See Biemer, *Die Lehre von der Tradition nach J. H. Newman,* pp. 39–40: 'Many Anglican theologians point out that when interpreting Scripture the Fathers are to be taken into account'. William Palmer (1803–1885), a sometime co-worker with Newman in the Oxford Movement and one of the leading ecclesiologists in the Anglican Church, says in his *A Treatise on the Church of Christ,* vol. 2, p. 10: 'We admit the necessity of both Scripture and Tradition to prove every article of faith'; and again on p. 47: 'I maintain, that Christianity cannot possibly admit that any doctrine established by universal tradition can be otherwise than divinely, infallibly true.' For a fuller discussion of Newman's position on tradition, see below, chapter 6.

with the idea of tradition as a source of authority a few years before, during the long vacation of 1824. At this time he was thrown together with Dr Hawkins, at the time vicar of St Mary's, the university church. He heard Hawkins preach his 'famous sermon' on tradition.[30] Recounting it later,[31] Newman remembers 'how long it appeared to' him; its impression upon him was not great.[32] But later, when he had 'read it and studied it as his gift, it made a most serious impression upon' him:[33]

> He lays down a proposition, self-evident as soon as stated, to those who have at all examined the structure of Scripture, *viz.* that the sacred text was never intended to teach doctrine, but only to prove it, and that, if we would learn doctrine, we must have recourse to the formularies of the Church . . . This view, most true in its outline, most fruitful in its consequences, opened upon me a large field of thought.[34]

That it had. He was now beginning to develop those first tappings in the direction of the teaching Church which had ·brought him through *Arians.* On the eve of the Oxford Movement, Perceval, Froude and Newman 'were all becoming conscious of the importance of primitive tradition, and the church as the tradition-bearing body'.[35]

Having formulated his position as above, Newman can then go on to say: 'We receive the Catholic doctrines as we receive the canon of Scripture, because, as our Article expresses it, "*of their authority*" there "*was never any doubt in the Church*".'[36] For him this is an 'external fact' which is not based 'on the powers of reasoning, however great, on the credit of no names, however imposing'.[37] This 'external fact' is the witness of the Church to those doctrines springing from the Apostolical College[38] and thus the only ones able to lay claim to orthodoxy. It is a witness far more imposing

---

30. Ward, *Young Mr. Newman,* p. 101; Arnold later viewed this sermon as the beginning of the Oxford Movement.
31. *Apol.,* p. 9.
32. Ward, *ibid.,* p. 101.
33. *Apol.,* p. 9.
34. *Apol.,* pp. 9–10.
35. Greenfield, *The Attitude of the Tractarians to the Roman Catholic Church,* Oxford, 1956, p. 96.
36. *Op. cit.,* p. 381.
37. *Ibid.*
38. *Ibid.*

than that proffered in a court of law; for it is 'the unanimous
tradition of all the churches to certain articles of faith'.[39]

This tradition consists mainly of the Fathers, those 'articulations'
of the primitive Church. But in what sense can they be said to form
a 'unanimous tradition'? Here Newman brings out his point in
all clarity; it is in the function of the Fathers in relation to the
Church and the faith that we are to look for their tradition:

> [it is] a point of doctrine which must be carefully insisted on.
> The Fathers are primarily to be considered as *witnesses,* not as
> *authorities*. They are witnesses of an existing state of things, and
> their treatises are, as it were, *histories*—teaching us, in the first
> instance, matters of fact, not of opinion. Whatever they them-
> selves might be, whether deeply or poorly taught in Christian
> faith and love, they speak, not their own thoughts, but the
> received views of their respective ages.[40]

This is essential to the thought being unfolded here. It is not in
themselves that the Fathers have their authority; it is in the fact that
they are witnesses to the faith and teaching of the Church in which
they are living. It is not their own thought, nor their own speculations, peculiar only to them, that gives their works and writings
such value and authority for our present day, indeed, for all time.
No; this 'matters not to the profit of their writings, nor again to
the authority resulting from them; for the *times* in which they
wrote of course *are* of authority, though the Fathers themselves
may have none'.[41]

Newman strikes here to the heart of his argument: it is the faith
which is all-important as the basis for doctrine; the *times*, i.e. the
living faith of those particular ages is what matters. The Fathers
receive, and only receive, their authority *as* witnesses to this living
faith. To base their authority on them, and not upon the faith of
which they are testimonials, would be to advance them as straw
against the wind.

Thus Newman brought his thought to a new point of maturity.
But he was soon to find a new opportunity to express himself on
this subject; other controversies were looming which proved again
to be catalysts for his searching mind.

39. *Ibid.,* p. 382.
40. *Ibid.,* p. 385—italics are Newman's.
41. *Ibid.,* pp. 385–6—italics are Newman's.

5

The Prophetical Office

At the beginning of the Tractarian Movement, a young student of Christ Church, Benjamin Harrison, had rallied to its support. He had a great interest in Semitic languages and, on the advice of Pusey, he went to Paris in the year 1834 to study Arabic under de Saci, one of the leading orientalists of the time. While there he came into contact with a most engaging cleric of the French Church: a certain Abbé Jager. After conversations on the state of relations between the Church of England and the Roman Church, Harrison found himself forced to return to England; but he and the Abbé promised to continue their discussions in the form of a correspondence to be published afterwards.[1] Thus formed, the plans were carried out.

Jager opened the controversy with a letter on Saturday, 30 August 1834, published in *Univers*. Harrison, taking fright at the quality of Jager's letter, replied, but at the same time asked Newman to step in for him; Newman agreed to do so. In the meantime the Abbé had already fired off two replies; Newman and Harrison huddled to plan their attack and it was agreed that Newman should take over completely.[2] The Abbé, however, without waiting for a reply (no one had told him that Newman, due to pressing business, would be unable to reply immediately), went ahead with the publication of a fourth letter, in two parts, on 7 and 8 November 1834. Newman's first reply finally got off on 25 December 1834, but only half of it was published, together with the full reply of the Abbé.

This action shattered the ground rules of the controversy, and the Abbé's handling of the whole affair became intolerable when

1. H. Tristram, 'In the Lists with the Abbé Jager' in *J. H. Newman—Centenary Essays*, London, 1945, pp. 203, 205–7.
2. *Ibid.*, pp. 208, 211. See also *Letters* II, p. 66.

Newman sent in the first part of his fourth reply, only to have the Abbé answer it without waiting for the second part and then publishing the whole correspondence in book form in this inchoate state. Under these conditions, Harrison and Newman decided to break off the correspondence.[3] Ostensibly, the cause of termination was the Abbé's running 'rough-shod over the terms of the agreement, but really because Newman felt that it would be fruitless to continue'.[4]

A treatment of this controversy, in regard to our theme, can be profitably put off until we come to an analysis of Newman's *Prophetical Office,* for, as he himself stated, 'Great portions of a correspondence which the writer commenced with a learned and zealous member of the Gallican Church are also incorporated in it.'[5] That is, Newman used much of what he had composed for his correspondence with the Abbé as a basis for the lectures he was in the process of delivering during the years 1834 and 1836. He 'arranged to deliver these lectures in a chapel which formed part of St. Mary's, known as Adam de Brome's chapel, so called after the founder of Oriel who was buried there. Hitherto, the place had been used as a sort of vestry.'[6]

This small side chapel—according to Dean Church a most 'desolate place'[7]—Newman turned into a lecture hall and there held the lectures which afterwards became his two books, *The Prophetical Office of the Church* and his *Lectures on Justification.*[8]

---

3. *Ibid.,* p. 219; see also *Orat.* vol. 18: Jager-Harrison-Newman, letters of Harrison to Newman, 2 and 24 June 1836; letter of Harrison to Jager, 11 July 1836. The published volume by Jager appeared under the title: *Le Protestantisme aux prises avec la Doctrine Catholique, ou controverses avec Plusiers Anglicans, Membres de l'Université d'Oxford, soutenues par M. L. Abbé Jager,* Paris, 1836. Newman's first reply comprises the third response of the volume (pp. 337–94); it is still to be seen among the Jager collection at Birmingham, in rough copy, in the original English; his second reply, the fourth response of the book, is missing, but his planned second part of this second reply is still in existence, in fine copy, running to thirty-three closely-written pages.
4. Tristram, 'In the Lists with the Abbé Jager', p. 219.
5. *V.M.* I, p. xi.
6. L. Bouyer, *Newman, his Life and Spirituality,* p. 163.
7. Dean Church, *The Oxford Movement,* p. 165.
8. The first delivered between 1834–1836, published in March of 1837; the latter held after Easter 1837, published March of 1838; further lectures held here by Newman were later turned into Tracts 83 and 85; see Dean Church, *The Oxford Movement,* p. 165.

Their influence at Oxford can be measured by Bouyer's description of the audience Newman attracted:

> An audience, which was constantly increasing in numbers and which included the cream of intellectual Oxford, wedged their way into this dingy chamber to listen to theological disputations, the like of which had never fallen from the lips of any Regius Professor.[9]

This first series, which later became the *Prophetical Office*, was in essence an attempt to provide a living example of the *via media,* the existence of which Newman himself (as we saw in the third chapter) knew to be, at the moment, theoretical. It was 'designed to bring out in what sense the Anglican Church was to be regarded as a reformed Church'; that is, Newman had to account for the fact that the Church of England was 'a Church apart, a separate entity, rejecting Roman Catholicism on the one hand, and Protestant Dissent on the other'.[10] In other words, Newman had to attempt a living example of his announced *via media*; he had already proclaimed it the goal of the Tractarians: could he really make it work?

Newman's attempt to realize his *via media* is important for our theme because in it he becomes fully conscious of the main problem facing him as an Anglican: the problem of authority.[11] In dealing with this problem he presented a one-sided consideration:

> The *via media* is in fact what has been later called 'the Catholic centre'. In dealing only with the Church as prophetical the lectures inevitably missed that centre, for the Church is the Mystical Christ working in the world with a three-fold anointing —that of prophet indeed, but also that of priest and . . . king.[12]

Only with the introduction Newman composed for its republication in 1877 does this work of his attain the necessary balance and harmony which we have seen to be his constant goal. Even in its incomplete form, however, it is seen by some as 'the most enduring work that Newman produced'.[13] As such it forms an essential link

9. Bouyer, *Newman, his Life and Spirituality,* p. 163.
10. *Ibid.,* p. 164.
11. *V.M.* I, pp. 126–7.
12. M. Ward, *Young Mr. Newman,* p. 262.
13. F. L. Cross, *John Henry Newman,* pp. 70–71.

in our study of his thought on the teaching office of the Church.

It would be impossible to discuss everything Newman brings out in his lectures on the prophetical office; the main point for our purposes is his attempt to set up a norm for the Church's teaching authority. In this respect his thought, being in an early stage of development, evinces a goodly amount of inconsistency.[14] We shall see him trying to form a basis for the authority of the Church, a basis which he hopes to win out of a confrontation with Rome and Protestantism. In the end it will become evident that he is beginning to swing towards an exaggeration of the authoritative aspect of the Church's teaching function, a swing which eventually ended in his going over to Rome.

Dean Church remarks that 'the point which Newman chose for his assault was indeed the key of the Roman position—the doctrine of infallibility. He was naturally led to this side of the question by the stress which the movement had laid on the idea of the Church as the witness and teacher of revealed truth.'[15]

In dealing with the question,

> He followed the great Anglican divines in asserting that there was true authority, varying in its degrees, in the historic Church . . . This view of the 'prophetical office of the Church' had the dialectical disadvantage of appearing to be a compromise, to many minds a fatal disadvantage. It got the name of *Via Media* . . . Yet it only answered to the certain fact, that in the early and undivided Church there was such a thing as authority, and there was no such thing known as Infallibility.[16]

But, as we will see, Newman had set up a false target; what he lambasted the Romans for, was not the Roman teaching of infallibility; and what he taught under the name of the indefectibility of the Church was, in fact, what the Roman Church claimed.[17] To give this indefectibility a foundation, he turned to antiquity, the age of the united and undivided Church; it did not 'in his eyes actually teach a creed, but it is the witness of the teaching of the undivided church, and he was ever listening to its voice'.[18]

14. See M. Connolly, *Newman's Anglican Concept of the Doctrinal Authority of the Church and its Relation to Infallibility*, p. 89.
15. Church, *The Oxford Movement*, pp. 210–13.
16. *Ibid.*
17. See Connolly, *op. cit.*, pp. 89–121; to my knowledge Connolly is the first author to recognize this discrepancy in Newman's argument.
18. Ward, *Young Mr. Newman*, p. 264.

Here we have once again Newman's thought on the Church as the witness to the faith insofar as it teaches. But, as events proved, it was a far too heavy load for antiquity to bear alone; and thus it collapsed, leaving him with nowhere to go but to Rome.[19] This collapse reveals a basic flaw in Newman's construction:

> It is a static appeal and as such renders the Church impotent face to face with progressive knowledge of the truth . . . if an appeal is made to antiquity as being more likely to provide us with the authentic tradition, where shall the line be drawn? . . . it was precisely this problem that broke Newman's belief in the Anglican *via media*.[20]

Let us now see how Newman advanced to this position. As we have observed, his basic concept of the Church as being able to teach insofar as it witnesses to the faith, and this in an organic unity of determining authority and determined witness, began, with the advent of the Oxford Movement, to appear in need of a much more solid underpinning than heretofore had seemed necessary. He had begun with a simple faith in the Fathers and their witness to antiquity; he now saw that this was not enough, that the Fathers themselves had to be shored up. The immediate impetus given to his efforts was the challenge of the Roman Church,[21] for 'Protestantism and Popery are real religions; no one can doubt about them; . . . but the *Via Media,* viewed as an integral system, has never had existence except on paper . . . it still remains to be tried whether what is called Anglo-Catholicism . . . is capable of being professed, acted on, and maintained on a large sphere of action and through a sufficient period'.[22]

This is the dilemma and there is no more basic way for it to be met than on the level of the teaching authority of the Church. For Newman, 'Christ alone is the Author and Finisher of faith in all its senses; His servants do but witness it, and their statements are then only valuable when they are testimonies, not deductions or conjectures.'[23] This is his foundation: only insofar as Christians and the Church give witness to what Christ has revealed is what they proclaim of any value for a life of faith.

19. See E. Rich, *Spiritual Authority in the Church of England,* p. 72.
20. *Ibid.,* p. 41.
21. *V.M.* I, pp. 4, 12.
22. *Ibid.,* pp. 16–17.
23. *Ibid.,* p. 52.

How are we to ascertain this witness, and know whether it is a
true witness or not? Newman counters: 'Catholicity, Antiquity,
and consent of Fathers, is the proper evidence of the fidelity or
Apostolicity of a professed Tradition.'[24] Here is Newman's point:
the Church, being divided and far from the original witness, is
bound by necessity to that early witness of antiquity for its own
basis of authority.[25] But there was another claimant to this position:
the Roman Church's concept of infallibility.

'The doctrine of the Church's Infallibility is made to rest upon
the notion, that any degree of doubt about religious truth is incompatible with faith, and that an external infallible assurance is
necessary to exclude doubt', says Newman.[26] His mistake here, as
he himself pointed out forty years later, was to confuse doubt of
belief and doubt of evidence. The former is naturally excluded,
as he admits later on in his lectures; the latter is not touched by
infallibility and is quite beside the point.[27] This—more an 'awareness that there was some "lack" in the rational grounds for belief'[28]
—makes clear Newman's misunderstanding of infallibility. Else-
where he can say of it: 'Unless we know the whole of any subject
we must have difficulties somewhere or other; and where they are
left, there we cannot possess infallible knowledge. To know some
things in any subject infallibly, implies that we know all things.'[29]

It is clear that Newman here ascribes a task to infallibility which
it does not have in anyone's understanding of it; namely, that it is
a faculty of omniscience, a gift of vision or illumination which aids
in knowing an object, i.e. revelation, in its fullest extent. In
Newman's presentation of it here, it is a faculty 'of universal knowledge'.[30] He must, obviously, reject such a notion as insufficient
for the task he had set himself: establishing the foundation of the
Church's teaching authority. For if one accepts this definition of
infallibility, then one must also conclude: 'to know all that is

24. *Ibid.*, p. 51.
25. See Rich, *Spiritual Authority in the Church of England,* p. 65: Newman's
attempt was to determine 'whether looking to Antiquity, so characteristic of
classical Anglicanism, could stand as a final court of appeal and whether the
whole *corpus* of Christian doctrine could be systematically built up upon it'.
26. *V.M.* I, p. 86.
27. Connolly, *op. cit.,* p. 100.
28. *Ibid.*
29. *V.M.* I, p. 89.
30. *Ibid.*, p. 91.

revealed with equal clearness, implies that there is nothing revealed.'[31] A most devastating argument, but unfortunately directed
against a non-existent foe.

What, then, was to be done? Newman still maintains that the
giving of witness is the supreme task of the Church; but this does
not help him in solving the one aspect of it which has been thrust
upon his attention at this moment: the witnessing aspect of the
Church's teaching function. He is well aware of this, as we have
seen; but what of the authoritative aspect, that side of the Church's
teaching task which determines and guides its giving of witness?
He has rejected what he feels to be the Roman solution of infallibility. And he admits 'a difficulty existing in the theory of the
Church's present authority'.[32] How this is to be met is the question.

Having rejected the Roman claim of infallibility as unequal to
the task of solving the dilemma of the Church's authority, he turns
next to the Protestants and their claim that 'each individual
Christian' is capable of 'ascertaining and deciding for himself from
Scripture what is Gospel truth, and what is not'.[33] But Newman
must reject this also. For him the Scriptures bear witness, not only
to the revelation of God, but to the Church.[34] This is so, because
'we appeal to Scripture as the word of God on the authority of the
Fathers'.[35] For Newman, 'Scripture was never intended to teach
doctrine to the many.'[36] He fully allows that 'the corpus of inter-
pretative tradition is the main practical *teacher* of doctrine, and that
the text of Scripture is not such, but only referred to for proof'.[37]
Scripture cannot interpret itself; it comes as a witness of God's
revelation but is not self-explanatory. Newman would not deny,
in the abstract, that an individual Christian might be able to draw
the truths of faith from Scripture; but the chances are against it.
A religious, wise and intellectually-gifted man, however, 'will
succeed: but who answers to this description but the collective
Church?'[38] Newman is once again back at his basic notion of the
whole Church's witness to the faith; but he now goes further: he

31. *Ibid.*, p. 90.
32. *Ibid.*, p. 127.
33. *Ibid.*, p. 128.
34. *Ibid.*, p. 132.
35. *Orat.*, Ms D 6₁, Newman's second part of his second reply to Jager, p. 18.
36. *V.M.* I, p. 158.
37. *Orat.*, Ms D 6₁, from Newman's first reply to Jager, p. 12.
38. *V.M.* I, p. 158.

would maintain that 'the Church Catholic may be truly said almost infallibly to interpret Scripture aright'.[39]

We can see here Newman's inconsistency in his use of infallibility: having just condemned it in its Roman dress, he here brings it forth as a tentative solution to his problem. It is the 'Church Universal'[40] which must testify to the truth. We notice here the train of Newman's thought: aware of the need for a basis to the Church's teaching authority, he cannot accept Roman infallibility, as he conceives of it, nor can he see the effectiveness of the Protestant claim to private judgment. On the other hand this confrontation has made him see the need for a more solid foundation than simply antiquity; for who is to decide 'whether the Church's doctrine is Apostolic, and how far Apostolic'?[41]

In this dilemma, Newman strikes forward to formulate a principle necessary for his foundation of the Church's authority:

> Not only is the Church Catholic bound to teach the Truth, but she is ever divinely guided to teach it; her witness of the Christian Faith is a matter of promise as well as of duty; her discernment of it is secured by a heavenly as well as by a human rule. She is indefectible in it, and therefore not only has authority to enforce, but is of authority in declaring it . . . The Church not only transmits the faith by human means, but has a supernatural gift for that purpose; that doctrine, which is true, considered as an historical fact, is true also because she teaches it.[42]

This is clearly at the heart of Roman teaching on the Church's infallibility, though Newman never uses that name and continues to call it the Church's indefectibility in doctrine.[43] Although he can, with the Protestants, accept Scripture as a source containing all of God's salvific truth,[44] he must, on the other hand, accept tradition's role of transmission: 'We do not, therefore, set up the Church against Scripture, but we make her the keeper and interpreter of Scripture.'[45]

But if, as above, Newman then ascribes an indefectibility to this

39. *Ibid.*
40. *Ibid.*, p. 171.
41. *Ibid.*, p. 189.
42. *Ibid.*, p. 190.
43. Connolly, *op. cit.*, p. 90.
44. *Orat.*, vol. 18, a note on the Jager–Newman correspondence.
45. *V.M.* I, p. 192.

Church bearing the Scriptures, 'what is the *ground* of this authority in the Church?' Newman answers: 'she speaks merely as the organ of the *Catholic* voice, and that the faith thus witnessed, is, as being thus witnessed, such, that whoso does not believe it faithfully, cannot be saved.'[46] Thus it is the faith, witnessed to by the whole Church, which constitutes the foundation for the Church's teaching authority.[47] It is on the basis of this faith, as so witnessed to by the Church precisely as catholic, that this Church is indefectible in its teaching of that faith.

Once again we have that organic unity of function in the Church's teaching task, but this time a new notion has been added, that of the Church's indefectibility in performing this task. What and how and where this indefectibility is in the Church, Newman does not know. His search for the answer will eventually take him to Rome.

At this moment, however, he is still searching for an adequate expression of his concept of the dialectic in the Church's teaching function. We saw above that he was able to see this notion analogously in the relation of the Scriptures to the tradition of the Church. Scripture, as the original witness, determines the Church and its life of faith; but tradition, in turn, determines Scripture in its witness insofar as the extent and limits of that witness are worked out by the Church in its tradition. Newman now introduces a new analogy to help his expression. In a letter to Froude dated 20 July 1835, he notes that 'the popular sense of Tradition is the voice of the body of the Church, the received system in the Church, the spirit circulating through it and poured out through the channels of its doctors and writers . . . which I may call *prophetical Tradition*.'[48] It is what St Paul called ' "the mind of the Spirit", the thought and principle which breathed in the Church, her accustomed and unconscious mode of viewing things, and the body of her received notions'.[49]

This tradition can be likened to the witness of the whole Church; it is a 'vast system, not to be embodied in one code or treatise, but consisting of a certain body of Truth, pervading the Church like an atmosphere . . . existing primarily in the bosom of the Church

46. *Ibid.*
47. See also *V.M.* I, pp. 230–31, 234.
48. Cited in J. Stern, 'Traditions apostoliques et Magistère selon J. H. Newman', p. 38.
49. *V.M.* I, p. 251.

itself'.[50] It is the life of the Church, to be found in its living faith, that daily witness to the Christ revealed by God.

In contrast to this may be placed the episcopal tradition, which consists of a 'collection of definite articles set apart from the first . . . formally and statedly enunciated and delivered from hand to hand . . . of the nature of a written document, and having evidence of its Apostolical origin the same in kind with that adducible for the Scriptures'.[51] Such a tradition, like Scripture, is original and determinate; yet it is lived and determined itself by that other kind of tradition called prophetical.

In such an analogy Newman was making clear once more his attempt to keep the organic balance in tune which he knew to exist in the Church's teaching function. Again and again he returns in these lectures to the fact of the Church's witnessing to the truth of revelation, whether in Scripture or borne down to our times by tradition.[52] He was led to do so by his recognition that Scripture, though 'the document of ultimate appeal in controversy, and the touchstone of all doctrine',[53] was yet insufficient by itself to present a full and complete witness to God's revelation in Christ. A guide was needed, and this guide for Newman was the Church bearing tradition.[54] But this guide itself needs a foundation for its action; in attempting to apply the rule of antiquity, Newman, though not seeing immediately how static such an application is, did feel vaguely that antiquity would not be able to bear up under the load. He felt the necessity of shoring it up with a notion delineating a divinely-given indefectibility in the teaching of doctrine.[55] It was to take him far.

---

50. *Ibid.*, p. 250.
51. *Ibid.*, p. 249.
52. See *ibid.*, pp. 268–9.
53. *Ibid.*, p. 309.
54. *Ibid.*, p. 274.
55. See above, footnotes 19, 20, 43.

6

Tradition and Scripture

This chapter cannot hope to be an exhaustive treatment of Newman's thought on the relationship of tradition to Scripture; this has already been presented in several outstanding works.[1] But it can serve the purpose of bringing us up to date on the development of Newman's thought to the year 1838. For it is the contention of this study that after 1838, with the advent of the Wiseman controversy and the crisis surrounding his conversion, a new development takes place in Newman's thought concerning our theme of the teaching function of the Church.

There is another change, too. It was at the end of 1838 and the beginning of 1839 that Newman felt himself to be at the height of his powers as regards the position he had been representing up to that time: 'In the spring of 1839 my position in the Anglican Church was at its height. I had supreme confidence in my controversial *status*, and I had a great and still growing success, in recommending it to others.'[2] From then on, his position in the Church of England declined. There are two writings of Newman from this period which will allow us to ascertain his position at this time and also provide a certain summing up of this first and all-important period in his thought. We now turn to the first of these.

In 1836 Oxford was rocked by a dispute over the Regius Chair of Theology. The details do not need to detain us long; the main point was that, in the appointment of a certain Dr Hampden to the chair, Newman and his companions saw an attempt to bring

1. Most notably in Günter Biemer's work (see Introduction, footnote 18, above). See also, for an extensive study of the place Scripture held in Newman's thought, J. Seynaeve, *Cardinal Newman's Doctrine on Holy Scripture*, Louvain, 1953, which contains much unpublished material; also H. Fries, 'J. H. Newmans Beitrag zum Verständnis der Tradition' in *Die mündliche Ueberlieferung*, M. Schmaus ed., Munich, 1957.
2. *Apol.*, p. 93.

undogmatic and latitudinarian views into the university. Instead of giving up all hope of being able to ascertain the doctrine of the Church because of a lack of proof, he maintained the principle that 'dogmatic formulas *do* require a guarantee higher than human reason can give: in the Catholic Church, her God-guaranteed actually operative power of infallible definition provides it'.[3] This was consonant with the advances in this direction Newman had made in his *Prophetical Office*, but the unavoidable conclusions were not immediately visible to him.[4]

In that same year Newman took up another controversy. There had appeared a small volume entitled *A Brothers' Controversy*, professing to be the exchange of letters between a Unitarian and his brother, a clergyman in the Church of England. Newman contends, in a note appended long after its composition, that the article he wrote in answer to this book was completed before the Hampden affair, and therefore was not to be counted as a product of that controversy. Nevertheless, it points up, just as that battle for dogmatic principles had done, a change in his thinking. With this article on tradition the turn for Newman had begun: the old Anglican standpoint could still be found in his controversy with the Abbé Jager, that the Church is infallible only insofar as it will never go under, but not in its internal commentary on revelation. Here, however, one can see the beginning, brought about by the confrontation which occurred in the *Prophetical Office*, of his ascribing this infallibility—his indefectibility—to the acts of the Church themselves.[5]

We have special justification for considering this writing of Newman's because he, commenting on it almost forty years later, felt that its doctrine was, on the whole, so consonant with what he would write on the subject then, that he forewent any corrective footnotes.[6] He begins by immediately rejecting Scripture as sufficient, on the whole, by itself; it is 'a test of revealed truth' but not 'its own interpreter, and that, as an historical fact, it has ever been furnished for individuals with an interpreter which is external to its readers and infallible, that is, with an ecclesiastical Tradition'.[7]

---

3. M. Ward, *Young Mr. Newman*, p. 294.
4. For an exact and very well documented account of the Dr Hampden affair, see O. Chadwick, *The Victorian Church* I, pp. 112–26.
5. G. Biemer, *Die Lehre von der Tradition nach J. H. Newman*, p. 113.
6. *Ess. C.H.* I, p. 137.
7. *Ibid.*, p. 103.

It is 'this Tradition, and not Scripture itself' which 'is our immediate and practical authority for such high doctrine'.[8]

Newman takes up here the thought already announced in his *Prophetical Office* and draws it out in a much stronger form: Scripture, by itself, even though it might contain, in some way, all truths for salvation, is unable to present these truths. There must be an organ capable of deciding what those truths are and then be in a position to present them. This is tradition, the tradition of the Church, which is supported by the infallibility of the Church. Newman has surrendered antiquity as a competent judge by itself and must take recourse, as was obvious in the last chapter, to an underpinning of infallibility for the authoritative side of the Church's teaching function.

The concentration, so lightly seen up to now, is swinging ever more to a study of the authoritative aspect of the Church's teaching activity. It is still determined, in its own act of determining, by the witness it is determining, i.e. Scripture and the faith of the Church, but Newman's view is for the most part narrowed on this one side. This tradition is the 'voice of Christendom in every time and place',[9] but it has 'an intrinsic, substantive authority, and a use collateral to Scripture',[10] and thus remains a necessity:

> To the millions for whom Redemption has been wrought, creeds and catechisms, liturgies and a theological system, the multitudinous ever-sounding voice, the categorical, peremptory incisiveness, the (so to say) full chime, of ecclesiastical authority, is a first necessity, if they are to realize the world unseen.[11]

This tradition itself is guaranteed by the 'number and the unanimity of its witnesses'; and Scripture verifies it, without, however, limiting it.[12] It has its force in the fact that it is 'the joint testimony of many local bodies, as independent witnesses to the separate existence in each of them, from time immortal, of that great dogma in which they found each other to agree'.[13]

Thus the authoritative side of the Church's teaching is itself a witness to its function of determining the witness of Scripture and

8. *Ibid.*
9. *Ibid.*, p. 112.
10. *Ibid.*, p. 118.
11. *Ibid.*, p. 121.
12. *Ibid.*, p. 126.
13. *Ibid.*, p. 128.

the faith of the Church. This act of witness performed by the Church in its authoritative aspect is in turn supported by the infallibility of that Church. This is, however, seen from the 'hierarchical side'; the witness of the *ecclesia docta* is no less needed in order for the Church to teach.[14] Newman is still aware of the balance necessary for a harmonious view of the Church's teaching function; but the weight of controversy is pushing him ever so slowly towards a concentration upon the one aspect of the authoritative determination of the Church's witness.

The second work of Newman's to be treated here is his Tract 85 of the *Tracts for the Times*.[15] Wilfrid Ward, composer of the great biography of the Cardinal, felt that 'some of his best thought' is contained in this work.[16] In fact Newman, with some of his thoughts on the composition of the New Testament, its dependence upon literary genres, and ruminations upon the nature of inspiration in light of such a text, did anticipate much of the foundational work done in this area by twentieth-century exegesis. But what interests us in this particular work is Newman's discussions on Scripture and tradition and his related remarks on the infallibility of the Church in such questions.

He makes the attempt to fulfill his 'need of finding dogma and determining its relation to Scripture'; this 'was his paramount concern if he was to remain an Anglican'.[17] But how is he to do this without falling either into latitudinarianism or being forced to go to Rome? '*Either* Christianity contains no definite message, creed, revelation, system, or whatever other name we give it . . . or again, though there is a true creed or system revealed, it is not revealed in Scripture, but must be learned collaterally from other sources.'[18]

There is, however, a third possibility: 'though there really is a true creed or system in Scripture, still it is not on the surface of Scripture, but is found latent and implicit within it, and to be

---

14. *Ibid.*, p. 130.
15. According to Dean Church (*The Oxford Movement*, p. 165), Newman held lectures, in the same side chapel where he had held those which went into the *Prophetical Office*, in the spring of 1838; these were then published in May of 1838 as Tract 85.
16. As cited by H. Tristram, 'On Reading Newman', p. 238.
17. R. Greenfield, *The Attitude of the Tractarians to the Roman Catholic Church*, p. 230.
18. *Dis. Arg.*, p. 127.

maintained only by indirect arguments, by comparison of texts, by inferences from what is said plainly, and by overcoming or resigning oneself to difficulties.'[19] There lies the problem: how are these doctrines, of which the creed or Christian system consists, to be determined?

Newman attempts, then, to work out a theory of tradition which will keep him from Rome. Starting on the basis that 'religion cannot but be dogmatic; it ever has been',[20] he points out that one has his choice: either say that religion's doctrines are outside of Scripture (with the Romanists), or can be inferred from Scripture (with Anglo-Catholicism). He understands here Roman tradition as being totally independent of Scripture, a completely differentiated source of doctrine; in contrast to this, he sees the Anglican concept of tradition anchored in the fact that tradition is a witness to Scripture and therefore justified in inferring from Scripture.[21]

This was a much more consequential step than Newman realized at the time, for although he still states that Scripture contains all truths necessary for salvation,[22] it is an empty statement. Then Tract 85 'shows him as having departed from the age-old attitude toward the Bible, which saw it as the primary source of Christian doctrine. Instead, he dissociated the whole system of Catholic doctrine from any but an incidental relationship to the Scriptures— the Faith was external to them, and did not derive its authority from them.'[23]

It is the Church which must witness, both to doctrine and to Scripture.[24] Thus,

For those who accepted Antiquity as normative in every way, the Church was invested with an authority not completely dependent upon scripture . . . Newman went beyond even this ground; in Tract 85, he came to the conclusion that tradition existed independent of Scripture and that the Fathers determined the canonicity of various writings in accordance with it. The Bible itself providentially contained all that was necessary to salvation, but derived its own authority from its witness to the

19. *Ibid.*
20. *Ibid.*, p. 134.
21. *Ibid.*, pp. 134–5.
22. *Ibid.*, pp. 149, 170.
23. Greenfield, *op. cit.*, p. 235.
24. *Dis. Arg.*, p. 215.

apostolic tradition. He was thus forced to accept the beliefs of the Church as a whole.[25]

Newman is once again at the beginning of his thought: it is the whole Church, witnessing, which brings a basis to the Church's teaching; this teaching is not simply opinion but is reality, as embodied in the living faith of the Church, its rites and usages.[26] At the same time he is clearing the road for a cautious acceptance of infallibility, insofar as he sees—what was not the case a few years before in the *Prophetical Office*[27]—that the doubt which he feels is necessarily bound up with faith, is a doubt 'as regards evidence'; not as regards the substance of faith.[28]

This prepares him for the task he began to see at this point in his thought; having been convinced of the necessity for a dogmatic religion since a youth, and such a conviction having been one of the guiding principles of the Oxford Movement,[29] he sees his fight as against a rationalism which will rob Christianity as a religion of its very substance.[30] However, 'the only way (for Newman) of holding the line against rationalism was to recognize the infallible guidance of the Holy Spirit within the life of the Church at all times. But once this principle was established, it was difficult to know where to draw the line.'[31] This was the problem he now faced.

25. Greenfield, *op. cit.*, p. 286.
26. *Dis. Arg*, p. 241.
27. See above, chapter 5.
28. *Dis. Arg.*, p. 248.
29. *Apol.*, pp. 48–9.
30. *Ibid.*, p. 48.
31. Greenfield, *op. cit.*, p. 313.

7

The Wiseman Controversy

The year 1838 ended for Newman with a foretaste of things to
come. He had written a recension of W. Palmer's 'Treatise on the
Church of Christ' for the *British Critic*; in it he began to be aware
of the problem which was about to arise for him.[1] Looking back
from a distance of some forty years, Newman can say that there is
very little in his article which he now, as a Catholic, would have
to correct.[2] He himself does not accept Palmer's version of the
branch theory of the churches, preferring to retain his own *via
media*.[3] In doing so, he brings up once more the objection he had
taken so lightly in his Tracts on the *via media*;[4] the problem of a
divided Christendom. Newman here still rejects infallibility as a
possible solution to this difficulty,[5] but he does see with much
greater clarity the problem posed by the disunity of the churches.

If the various churches in present-day Christianity all claim to
be the one Church of Christ, and if they all claim heritage with the
apostolic Church of antiquity, then the question automatically
poses itself: 'whether local bodies which have separated from each
other can possibly be part of one and the same body; for if they
cannot, we shall be driven perforce either to deny that there is a
Catholic Church, or else to deny either the Roman Communion
or our own to be part of it.'[6]

Newman attempts to get around this touchy question by posing
the *via media* in the form of a theory of fundamentals: it maintains
that 'the faith being the foundation of the Church as well as of the

1. In the *British Critic*, October 1838, pp. 347–72; now to be found in *Ess. C.H.* I,
pp. 179–221.
2. *Ess. C.H.* I, p. 216.
3. *Ibid.*, pp. 209–10.
4. See above, chapter 3, footnote 27; *Dis. Arg.*, p. 6.
5. *Ess. C.H.* I, p. 186.
6. *Ibid.*, p. 197.

individual', it follows that 'the individual is bound to obey the Church, only so far as the Church holds to the faith'.[7] This is the theory of fundamentals; its peculiar characteristic is that it 'supposes the Truth to be entirely objective and detached, not lying hid in the bosom of the Church as if one with her, clinging to her and (as it were) lost in her embrace, but as being sole and unapproachable as on the Cross or at the Resurrection, with the Church close by, but in the background'.[8]

He wants thus to escape from the problem of the divided churches by taking refuge in a truth which is, in a way, a third pole, upon which one could cling if the unity of the Church catholic were to crumble—which in fact has occurred. This, however, takes him out of the frying pan and into the fire, because in this schema 'the chief difficulty obviously lies in determining what *is* the fundamental faith'.[9] This means that the problem of church unity is of a sudden intimately bound up with that of church authority. The more one searches for authority in the Church's teaching function, all the more necessary will church unity appear. And the more one tries to live with the disunity among the churches, all the more will the Church's teaching authority tend to dissolve. As Froude wrote to Newman:

> Your trumpery principle about Scripture being the sole rule of faith in *fundamentals* (I nauseate the word), is but a mutilated edition of the Protestant principle of the Bible and the Bible only, without the breadth and the axiomatic character of the original.[10]

This put Newman square in the firing line: if continued in this fashion, he could very easily end up in the camp of dreaded liberalism; if he were, however, to go in the direction of a more flexible and living authority, he would end in Rome.

In April of 1839 Newman wrote an article in the *British Critic* on 'The State of Religious Parties'.[11] He himself says that it best describes his mind at that moment.[12] Looking back from over

7. *Ibid.,* p. 209.
8. *Ibid.,* pp. 209–10.
9. *Ibid.*
10. As quoted by Newman, *ibid.*
11. Now in *Ess. C.H.* I, pp. 263–308, under the title: 'Prospects of the Anglican Church'.
12. *Apol.,* p. 94.

twenty years after the fact, he is quite struck by what this small article reveals:

> It contains the last words which I ever spoke as an Anglican to Anglicans. It may now be read as my parting address and valediction, made to my friends. I little knew it at the time.[13]

The article reviews the state of affairs in the Church of England, and ends with an analysis of the future prospects for Anglo-Catholicism. In discussing the state of the Church of England, and thus also the Oxford Movement, Newman was brought to remarks covering the *via media*, understood not as 'a servile imitation of the past, but such a reproduction of it as is really new, while it is old'.[14]

Still clinging to antiquity as the support needed to prop up the Church in its authoritative presentation of the truth, in the form of the *via media*, Newman dismisses liberalism as a serious contender for the hearts and minds of members of the English Church; the formularies of Anglo-Catholicism, resting as they do on antiquity and the Fathers, will prove more than able to turn away any inroads made by it.[15] But in pleading the *via media*, he was aware that the situation in which the Anglican Church stood at the moment was not real, and that whatever would come after would be *real*, and something would come.[16] Then the task will be:

> ... to look for some Via Media which will preserve us from what threatens, though it cannot restore the dead. The spirit of Luther is dead; but Hildebrand and Loyola are still alive ... Would you rather have your sons and daughters members of the Church of England, or of the Church of Rome?[17]

Here it is in a nutshell; the moment is critical, both for Newman and for the Church of England.

It is no wonder that, in looking back, Newman called his words here the last which he spoke 'as an Anglican to Anglicans'. For he thought at the time that he had taken care of the matter; but 'while I was thus speaking of the future of the Movement, I was in truth winding up my accounts with it, little dreaming that it was so to be;—while I was still, in some way or other, feeling about

13. *Ibid.*
14. *Ibid.,* p. 101.
15. *Ess. C.H.* I, p. 294.
16. *Apol.,* pp. 102–3; *Ess. C.H.* I, pp. 305–7.
17. *Ess. C.H.* I, pp. 306–7.

for an available *Via Media*, I was soon to receive a shock which was to cast out of my imagination all middle courses and compromises for ever'.[18] It is to this that we now turn.

In the summer of 1839 Newman began to research the history of the Monophysites. This was about the middle of June; by the end of August the crisis had broken upon him.[19] In working out the positions held by the various groups involved in the Council of Chalcedon, Newman had found in it the 'Christendom of the sixteenth and the nineteenth centuries reflected'.[20] It looked like this:

> I saw my face in that mirror, and I was a Monophysite. The Church of the *Via Media* was in the position of the Oriental communion, Rome was where she now is; and the Protestants were the Eutychians.[21]

It was, as he said, as if 'the shadow of the fifth century was on the sixteenth'.[22] In looking at the heresy of the fifth century, Newman had seen the very same position, as occupied by the Anglican Church since the sixteenth, being filled by the Orientals, the *via media* of the Council of Chalcedon.

Up to this time, as we have seen, Newman retained his theory that antiquity, the Church of the Fathers, was the basis for the teaching activity of the Church.[23] But with his study of Chalcedon, he had received a blow from another direction, and things began to change.[24] His previous position can be described as follows:

> In Mr. Newman's view of the debate between England and Rome, he had all along dwelt on two broad features, *Apostolicity* and *Catholicity*, likeness to the Apostolic teaching, and likeness to the uninterrupted unity and extent of the undivided Church; and of those two features he found the first signally wanting in Rome and the second signally wanting in England.[25]

18. *Apol.*, p. 104.
19. It is not the purpose of our study to give a complete account of this incident in Newman's life; for a more extensive and very incisive telling, see H. Fries, 'Die Dogmengeschichte des 5. Jahrhunderts im theologischen Werdegang von J. H. Newman' in *Das Konzil von Chalkedon* III, A. Grillmeier and H. Bacht ed., pp. 421–54.
20. *Apol.*, p. 114.
21. *Ibid.*
22. *Ang. Diff.* I, p. 388.
23. See Fries, *op. cit.*, p. 425.
24. *Ibid.*, p. 428.
25. Dean Church, *The Oxford Movement*, p. 228; see also, *Apol.*, p. 106.

But now he was unsettled. In a letter written some years afterwards, he describes the crisis:

> ... I found more matter for serious thought in that history (of the Monophysites) than in anything I had read. ... I found the Eastern Church under the superintendence (as I may call it) of Pope Leo. I found that *he* had made the Fathers of the Council unsay their decree and pass another, so that (humanly speaking) we owe it to Pope Leo at this day that the Catholic Church holds the true doctrine. I found that Pope Leo based his authority on St. Peter ... I found there was a large middle party as well as an extreme. There was a distinct *Via Media* ... in a word I found a complete and wonderful parallel, as if a prophecy, of the state of the Reformation controversy, and that we were on the anti-Catholic side ... now I had got *a key*, which interpreted large passages of history which had been locked up from me. I found everywhere one and the same picture, prophetic of our present state, the Church in communion with Rome decreeing, and heretics resisting.[26]

He has found the Anglican community to be, historically speaking, in the position of schism; for if the Anglicans accepted the teaching of the Council of Chalcedon as binding—and they did[27]—then their own position had to be in line with that Council. But Newman had just seen that they 'were on the anti-Catholic side'; and even more astounding:

> I saw that, if the early times were to be my guide, the Pope had a very different place in the Church from what I had supposed. When this suspicion had once fair possession of my mind, and I looked on the facts of the history for myself, the whole English system fell about me on its sides, the ground crumbled under my feet, and in a little time I found myself in a very different scene of things.[28]

Perhaps there was an instance in ecclesiastical authority which Newman had not seen up to now; perhaps the pope had made sovereign and authoritative decisions;[29] perhaps the pope was in

26. Newman to Mrs Froude, 5 April 1844, as quoted in M. Ward, *Young Mr. Newman*, pp. 462–3; see also, *Correspondence of J. H. Newman with J. Keble, etc.*, pp. 16–25.
27. Fries, *op. cit.*, p. 428.
28. *Correspondence of J. H. Newman with J. Keble, etc.*, p. 17.
29. Fries, *op. cit.*, p. 433.

possession of that gift of infallibility promised the Church. Writing to Keble in 1843, Newman admits as much; 'In June and July 1839, near four years ago, I read the Monophysite Controversy, and it made a deep impression on me, which I was not able to shake off, that the Pope had a certain gift of infallibility, and that communion with the See of Rome was the divinely intended means of grace and illumination.'[30]

Newman scarcely had time to recover from this moment of crisis, when another arrived: 'Hardly had I brought my course of reading to a close, when the *Dublin Review* of that same August was put into my hands, by friends who were more favourable to the cause of Rome than I was myself. There was an article in it on the "Anglican Claim" by Dr. Wiseman... It was on the Donatists, with an application to Anglicanism.'[31] It did not seem to bother Newman at first;[32] but his friend, who had shown him the article to begin with, 'pointed out the palmary words of St. Augustine, which were contained in one of the extracts made in the *Review*, and which had escaped my observation. "Securus judicat orbis terrarum." He repeated these words again and again, and, when he was gone, they kept ringing in my ears.'[33] And with good reason, for they opened up a new vista for Newman's thought as regards our theme. It brought to the fore the thought that perhaps antiquity was not enough; that another source of authority could be expected, nay, must be expected; and that the case of Leo at Chalcedon gained even more clarity in the light of Augustine's words.[34]

Newman was so excited, as he tells us, because the fact he had found in the Monophysite controversy—'that churches in isolation were always wrong in primitive times' and which he had felt as a presumption against the Anglican claims[35]—was here represented as a *principle and rule* in those same ages'.[36] The same parallel was

---

30. *Correspondence of J. H. Newman with J. Keble, etc.*, p. 219.
31. *Apol.*, p. 116; the article by Wiseman is to be found in *Dublin Review* 7 (1839) 139–80, entitled: 'The Anglican Claim of Apostolic Succession'. According to J. Stern ('Traditions apostoliques et Magistère selon J. H. Newman', p. 49): 'It was anonymous, as were many authors' articles in the *Review*, but there was no mystery as to the identity of the author.' It was Wiseman.
32. *Apol.*, p. 116.
33. *Ibid.*
34. Fries, *op. cit.*, p. 437; see also *Apol.*, p. 117.
35. *Correspondence of J. H. Newman with J. Keble, etc.*, p. 26.
36. *Ibid.*

there, which he had drawn between the Anglicans and the Mono-physites; and more: 'the *fact* of separation was reckoned anciently as decisive against the body separated.'[37] Thus it was driven home to him once more: 'we were in a state of schism.'[38] His antiquity had not borne up under the blows of the Fathers themselves; in this contradiction the *via media* came tumbling down about his ears.

In order to combat the situation, he wrote his article on 'The Catholicity of the Anglican Church'.[39] He had confessed to his friend Rogers that he had received 'the first real hit from Romanism',[40] and he had to answer it: 'My first business then, was to examine this question carefully, and see, whether a great deal could not be said after all for the Anglican Church, in spite of its acknowledged short-comings.'[41] In this article Newman had to defend himself, and the Anglican community, against the charge of schism; he maintains that they may be in schism, but still be in the possession of the apostolic succession, and thus of divine grace.[42] The charge of schism rests on the supposition that the Anglicans are not in possession of the note of catholicity, which the Roman communion does possess, and which is necessary for full participation in the one Church of Christ.[43]

The problem is quite clear: the Anglicans insist upon antiquity, i.e. ancient consent as the standard of faith; the Romans maintain that universal consent is the true standard of faith.[44] But this still proves surmountable; the Church of England is only in schism if the Roman contention is true; and this is only so, if one grants their presumption, that the Church has the power 'to add to the faith'.[45] Here is the crux of the matter. Though Newman had granted that Anglicanism *was* in a state of schism precisely because of the lack of the note of catholicity, he now is trying to 'conquer this feeling' and put it out of his mind.[46] His argument takes the following form:

37. *Ibid.*
38. *Ibid.*, p. 219.
39. *Ibid.*, pp. 219, 276; the article itself appeared in the *British Critic* 27 (January 1840) pp. 40–88; it is now to be found in *Ess. C.H.* II, pp. 1–73; according to Newman it was written 'in answer to the article of Dr. Wiseman, which (I acknowledge) is striking' (*Letters* II, p. 266).
40. *Letters* II, p. 256.
41. *Apol.*, p. 129.
42. *Ess. C.H.* II, p. 3.
43. *Ibid.*, p. 4.
44. *Ibid.*, p. 6.
45. *Ibid.*, p. 12.
46. *Correspondence of J. H. Newman with J. Keble, etc.*, p. 219.

according to the branch theory, it is clear that catholicity, i.e. ecclesial unity, is granted insofar as one is apostolic, i.e. in the line of a common descent from one original.[47] If the essence of a church 'consists in her descent from the Apostles, such an absorption, or such a suspension of intercommunion with other branches, as is consequent upon it, may be expedient or inexpedient, allowable or culpable, but does not touch the life of the Church, or compromise the tenure of its privileges'.[48]

Newman is here representing the Anglican theory of unity which is anchored, not in the Church as universal, but in the bishop in his diocese as a type of Christ: 'he was to the Church on earth what God was to the Church in Heaven.'[49] It is the separation from the particular bishop which is the cause of schism, not a separation from an abstract 'universal' church: '. . . for if the bishop be Christ's representative, the effect of separating from the bishop is thus simply shown to be a separating from Christ.'[50] This is so because of the 'simple principle that Bishops everywhere, and not the Pope, are the elementary centres of unity'.[51]

Thus the question is even more clearly and dramatically posed:

> Now the question between us and the Romanists is, whether *the* Church spoken of, in which is salvation, is the particular and local Church everywhere (or, again, the abstract Church of which the local is its realization under the bishop), or whether it is the literal and actual extended communion of all Christians everywhere viewed as one body under the supremacy of the Pope.[52]

Newman had, in the light of Augustine's words, already felt the power of authority provided by such a living, universal communion; the idea had already flashed through his mind that this was indeed the ultimate foundation for the Church's gift of teaching,[53] but here he is putting it from his mind and posing the question once anew, to see if he cannot defend himself against it.

47. *Ess. C.H.* II, p. 18.
48. *Ibid.,* p. 20.
49. *Ibid.,* p. 27.
50. *Ibid.,* p. 28.
51. *Ibid.,* p. 29.
52. *Ibid.*
53. See above, footnotes 34 and 35.

And he does. He opts for the former of the proposed solutions:

> Schism then, in its formal sense, is not the separation of Church
> from Church, which when separated from each other are still
> perfect, but laceration of the organic structure of the particular
> or local Church itself.[54]

He sums up this Anglican theory of ecclesiastical unity by saying
that 'each Church is naturally independent of every other; each
bishop an autocratic channel of grace, and ultimate centre of unity;
and that unions of see with see are only matters of ecclesiastical
arrangement; further, that no jurisdiction but the episcopal is of
divine right'.[55]

He has put the shadow of the fifth century, which for a brief
spell lay upon the sixteenth, from him; and in the process, as he
himself noted some forty years later,[56] comes perilously close, in
his effort to save his situation, to making the Church an invisible
union. Thus he maintains that the union existing between churches
is not a 'political' one—this word to be taken in its widest sense—
but a 'brotherly' one, one in spirit only. But if the unity of the
Church is, for all practical purposes, spiritual and invisible, does
that not lead eventually to an 'invisible' Church?

It is upon this dilemma, which would have wiped out any
authoritative teaching act of the Church, that Newman's theories
of union and schism finally broke. For if one maintains, as he does,[57]
that catholicity is the essence of union within the Church, then he
must eventually see that such a catholicity cannot only be based
upon a common denominator, i.e. antiquity, the Church of the
Fathers; it must also be a reality. He tries, this time, to evade this
problematic by maintaining that, though such communion is
ideally necessary for the Church's perfection, in practice the
Church can also exist in an imperfect state, e.g. as now. But this
was a much too flimsy support for the task Newman demanded
of the Church, i.e. to be the 'pillar and ground of truth'. He finally
turns the thought of Augustine aside with the remark that it would
surely be unreasonable 'to make a saying of St. Augustine the

---

54. *Ess. C.H.* II, p. 30.
55. *Ibid.*, p. 32.
56. *Ibid.*, p. 34, footnote.
57. *Ibid.*, p. 36.

turning-point of our religion, and to dispense with all other truths in order that we maintain this in the letter'.[58]

But it was not a case of throwing all other principles to the wind; Newman had already seen the words of Augustine in another light:

> They decided ecclesiastical questions on a simpler rule than that of Antiquity; nay, St. Augustine was one of the prime oracles of Antiquity; here then Antiquity was deciding against itself. What a light was hereby thrown upon every controversy in the Church! . . . the deliberate judgment, in which the whole Church at length rests and acquiesces, is an infallible prescription and a final sentence against such portions of it as protest and secede . . . the words of St. Augustine struck me with a power which I had never felt from any words before . . . By those great words of the ancient Father, interpreting and summing up the long and varied course of ecclesiastical history, the theory of the *Via Media* was absolutely pulverized.[59]

These words of Augustine had proved even more real at the Council of Chalcedon than in the heresy of Donatism; they showed—and the Council showed—that the Church not only had the task of giving witness, but also possessed the power to make decisions, binding decisions, on the basis of earlier witnesses. Such a binding decision, however, is not possible without an authority, which can function authentically, infallibly and binding, i.e. the authority of an infallible Church.[60]

Newman has begun to reap the fruits of his thought as presented over three years earlier in the *Prophetical Office*. The Church is infallible in its universal witness to its living faith; it is this active catholicity which completes the witness of antiquity, which without such a completion would remain dry and sterile. But the full harvest was not to be so easily gathered; the writing of the 'Catholicity of the Anglican Church' stilled his mind,[61] and 'for two years it quieted' him.[62] Then the storm broke once more.

58. *Ibid.,* p. 43; it is interesting that Newman, in the light of hindsight, calls this remark his 'second thoughts' on Augustine's *securus judicat orbis terrarum.* His first thoughts on it, he says, are contained in *Apol.,* p. 117: 'A mere sentence struck me with a power, which I never had felt from any words before.' He then goes on to say that his 'third thoughts came back to his first'; see *Ess. C.H.* II, p. 43, footnote.
59. *Apol.,* p. 117.
60. Fries, 'Die Dogmengeschichte des 5. Jahrhunderts im theologischen Werdegang von J. H. Newman', p. 438.
61. *Correspondence of J. H. Newman with J. Keble, etc.,* p. 219.
62. *Ibid.,* p. 276.

8

The Tract 90 Affair

Two years of respite had been given Newman by his article on the 'Catholicity of the Anglican Church'; and then came Tract 90.[1] Written to take the pressure off himself and others in the Movement, this last of the *Tracts for the Times* endeavored to place a catholic interpretation upon the 39 Articles of the Church of England. These Articles had been composed in the sixteenth century as a basis for the Church of England's independent stance within Christianity; not only the clergy, but also students at the English universities had to subscribe to them.[2]

There had always been a tradition of liberal interpretation as applied to the Articles,[3] but even Oxford was not prepared for Newman's distinction between Roman Catholic and Catholic: the words were normally interchangeable, and the immediate impression of Newman's attempted interpretation was that the barriers were down to the acceptance of Roman Catholic doctrine in the Anglican Church.[4] It is not to our purpose to go into the whole and quite complicated history of this affair; it will suffice if we first analyse Newman's thought as presented in the Tract, and then take up the resulting action brought about by its appearance.

Tract 90 appeared on 27 February 1841 and within a week all England was in an uproar—which had not been anticipated by Newman at all.[5] The opinions ranged from thinking it was an attempt to join England with Rome, to holding it to be a dastardly example of sophistry.[6] Newman could not understand all the furor. For him the 39 Articles were a stumbling block—not for him

1. For an excellent account, see O. Chadwick, *The Victorian Church* I, pp. 181–9.
2. M. Ward, *Young Mr. Newman*, p. 366.
3. Chadwick, *The Victorian Church* I, p. 181.
4. *Ibid.*, p. 183.
5. Ward, *Young Mr. Newman*, p. 370; see also *Letters* II, p. 292.
6. Chadwick, *The Victorian Church* I, p. 188.

personally, but for the catholic tendencies of the Movement.[7] Why? Because an objection urged against the Anglican communion maintained that the 39 Articles constituted a positive note against Anglicanism:

> Anglicanism claimed to hold, that the Church of England was nothing else than a continuation in this country (as the Church of Rome might be in France or Spain,) of that one Church of which in old times Athanasius and Augustine were members. But, if so, the doctrine must be the same; the doctrine of the Old Church must live and speak in Anglican formularies, in the 39 Articles.[8]

But, was this the case? Did it live on in the 39 Articles?

> Yes, it did; that is what I maintained; it did in substance, in a true sense. Man had done his worst to disfigure, to mutilate, the old Catholic Truth; but there it was, in spite of them, in the Articles still. It was there,—but this must be shown. It was a matter of life and death to us to show it.[9]

Newman contended that such an interpretation had always been in the Articles, but that it had never been 'publically recognized'; the interpretation of the moment was strictly Protestant.[10] It had to be interpreted by the one agency capable of doing so: 'the Church Catholic'.[11]

What had always been taught by the Church catholic *had* to be present in the Anglican Church too, if it was to preserve its place as a genuine branch of that one Church catholic.[12] If such were the case, then it was the duty of its members 'ever to profess what the Universal Church had from the beginning professed, and nothing else, and nothing short of it . . . inasmuch as the Divine Lord of the Church watched over all her portions, and would not suffer the Anglican or any portion to commit itself to statements which could not fairly and honestly be made to give forth a Catholic meaning'.[13]

This is the shadow reappearing of Augustine's claim that it is

7. *Apol.*, p. 129.
8. *Ibid.*
9. *Ibid.*, pp. 129–30.
10. *Ibid.*
11. *V.M.* II, p. 261.
12. *Ibid.*
13. *Ibid.*, p. 262.

9

A Development of Doctrine

Though Newman found himself by the end of 1841 on his death-bed as an Anglican, he was unable to make the final break for almost four years. By this time he had worked out his now famous theory of the development of doctrine, and it provided the certainty of mind he needed in order to proceed with the rupture.[1]

By 1843 Newman had taken two important steps; first of all, he issued a recantation of 'all the hard things' he had said against Rome; secondly, he resigned his living as pastor of St Mary's, the university church.[2] Retiring to live at Littlemore, the small community shed he had set up some three to four miles from Oxford, near the small parish which had been connected to St Mary's, he devoted himself to the principle of development which had been in his mind for years.[3] He made it the subject of his last University Sermon in February of 1843,[4] and by 1844 was in a position to say that 'I am very far *more* sure that England is in schism, than that the Roman additions to the Primitive Creed may not be developments, arising out of a keen and vivid realizing of the Divine Depositum of faith.'[5]

He began his *Essay on the Development of Doctrine* in early 1845 and worked at it all through that summer into October. But in working on his book, his difficulties seemed to dissipate so quickly that he 'resolved to be received, and the book remains in the state in which it was then, unfinished'.[6] On the night of 8 October 1845,

1. For an excellent study of Newman's Theory of Development, see O. Chadwick, *From Boussuet to Newman—The Idea of Doctrinal Development*, Cambridge, 1957; the best account of his conversion still remains his *Apologia pro vita sua*; for an account that attempts to place it in its setting, see M. Ward, *Young Mr. Newman*, and L. Bouyer, *Newman, his Life and Spirituality*.
2. *Apol.*, p. 200.
3. *Ibid.*, p. 197.
4. *U.S.*, pp. 312–51.
5. *Correspondence of J. H. Newman with J. Keble, etc.*, p. 219.
6. *Apol.*, p. 234.

he wrote to several friends that Father Dominic, the Passionist, was to come to Littlemore that night, and that he would ask him to receive him into the 'One Fold of the Redeemer'.[7] The next day, the ninth of October, John Henry Newman, having spent exactly half his life in the Church of England, went out from his spiritual mother and entered into the communion of Rome.

For our purposes the major theme of importance in this episode of Newman's life is his working out of papal infallibility. In 1843, as we have seen, Newman, due to his studies of the Council of Chalcedon and the role played in it by Leo the Great, thought enough of the pope's position that he could cautiously speak of 'a certain gift of infallibility' in the possession of the pope.[8] But how and in what manner this was to be delineated did not become apparent to him until he had worked out his *Development of Doctrine*. As we shall see, his presentation of this thought led to the exclusion of the role played also by the whole Church precisely as universal; the pope's position within the Church's teaching function was properly worked out, but left isolated and exaggerated in the lack of balance which obtains when the role of the whole Church in its witness is not kept in harmony with that played by the authoritative aspect.

The basic change which first becomes obvious is that antiquity, until now Newman's focal point, vacates its place and is replaced by an infallible teaching office located in Rome.[9] He begins his analysis by pointing out that an infallible authority of some sort is antecedently to be expected[10]—that is, granted that developments of some sort are to take place. For there must be some way of deciding between a false development and a true one.[11] Since, however, the developments, not yet worked out during their period of gestation, cannot carry their own authentication with themselves, whatever authoritative instance is expected must be external to the developments themselves.[12]

Granted the giving of a revelation—this being the essence of Christianity—Newman maintains that, on the analogy of creation in nature, there must be a principle of authority present to care for

7. *Letters* II, pp. 418–19.
8. *Correspondence of J. H. Newman with J. Keble, etc.*, p. 219.
9. G. Biemer, *Die Lehre von der Tradition nach J. H. Newman*, p. 152.
10. *Devel.*, p. 96.
11. *Ibid.*, p. 97.
12. *Ibid.*

the preservation of the revelation.[13] 'As creation argues continual governance, so are Apostles harbingers of Popes.'[14] According to Newman, the essence of all religion is obedience and authority; the very fact that revealed religion is dependent upon a given— namely the objective revelation of God—argues for the existence of an objective authority:[15]

> The supremacy of conscience is the essence of natural religion; the supremacy of Apostle, or Pope, or Church, or bishop is the essence of revealed . . . what conscience is in the system of nature, such is the voice of Scripture, or of the Church, or of the Holy See, as we may determine it, in the system of revelation.[16]

Looking at history, then, after having established the expectation for such an authority, Newman can find only one claimant to this mighty office: the Church of Rome in the person of its popes. 'Some authority there must be if there is a revelation given, and other authority there is none but she.'[17] For him there is no *via media* possible any more; he has now, with his theory of the development of doctrine, acknowledged the existence of a real teaching office in the Church.[18] There can be no basis for truth without an organ of truth;[19] since the Church is the 'pillar and ground of truth', it must be endowed with such an organ.

Viewing the question historically, Newman finds his search for papal supremacy guided by two points. His first is the probability for such a supremacy, which, as we have seen, is for him a certainty. The argument that such a phenomenon is not to be found in the early Church, does not bother him; on the basis of development it is to be expected that such a doctrine would not make its appearance until it had been challenged and forced into the open.[20] Besides, 'supposing there be otherwise good reason for saying that the Papal supremacy is part of Christianity, there is nothing in the early history of the Church to contradict it'.[21]

His other point of guidance is the actual state of the Church in

13. *Ibid.*, p. 103.
14. *Ibid.*
15. *Ibid.*
16. *Ibid.*, pp. 103–4.
17. *Ibid.*, p. 106.
18. Biemer, *Die Lehre von der Tradition nach J. H. Newman*, p. 152.
19. *Devel.*, p. 107.
20. *Ibid.*, pp. 159–60.
21. *Ibid.*, p. 163.

its post-Nicene era. It was essential that the unity of the Church be preserved; otherwise it would have disintegrated under the blows of heresy, schism and war. The very historical situation demanded such an office as that of the pope. 'It must be so; no Church can do without its Pope.'[22] Newman then introduces a series of texts from the fourth and fifth centuries which he considers more than ample in their testimony to the position of papal supremacy at that time. His only question is whether such testimony is enough to let through the light, dim though it be, from the very beginning; this question, if one takes his theory of development into consideration, has already been answered: it is antecedently probable that such a development will take place; historically, it did take place; therefore, the initial given has been proven. For Newman there is no doubt any more; his mind, which had craved for certainty in its many years of wandering through Christian doctrine, at length was at peace in the firm possession of an organ of truth, an organ which makes the Church truly 'the pillar and ground of truth'.

Newman takes up one more topic useful to his discussion of papal supremacy, the Monophysite heresy. We have seen how this had unsettled him six years before, and how he had then gained his first insight leading towards the infallibility of the Church, and hence of the pope.[23] He now takes up its history again, especially the Council of Chalcedon, and finds there the dominant role played by Leo, precisely as pope.[24] He sees again, but this time in full clarity, 'the principle of the Church's infallibility, i.e. the power and commission to decide, in an authentic and binding way, the what, the how and the fact of revelation'.[25] Now he sees something else; there is something new there which he had failed to discern the last time he went over this history. It is the fact that 'this commission and this gift were concentrated in the uncontested teaching authority of the Roman pope, who can decide a disputed question authoritatively and sovereignly'.[26]

With this certainty, Newman leaves the Anglican Church and goes over to Rome. His views on the teaching function of the Church have concentrated themselves in the office of the pope, to the practical exclusion of the role played by the rest of the Church.

22. *Ibid.*, p. 164.
23. *Correspondence of J. H. Newman with J. Keble, etc.*, p. 219.
24. See *Devel.*, pp. 286–308.
25. Fries, 'Die Dogmengeschichte des 5. Jahrhunderts . . .'. p. 440.
26. *Ibid.*

Theoretically the balance is still there, but Newman does not have it on the top of his mind; it is buried and ruminating in his depths, and it will take another crisis to bring it forth once more.[27]

27. In 1847 Newman wrote a paper in Latin to Perrone, the Jesuit theologian in Rome, delineating his ideas on development, to see if they, in the eyes of a well-known theologian of the Roman school, were acceptable. It is to be found in *Gregorianum* 16 (1935) pp. 402–47. Newman here, interestingly enough, presents a view which has the prophetical tradition in the Church shade off into the episcopal tradition (pp. 413–15); this would be a further sign of his concentration on the authoritative side of the Church's teaching function, to the exclusion of the role played by the witness of the whole Church. In the *Prophetical Office* he attempted to hold these two sources of teaching authority in the Church in a harmony which would grant each full room for exercising its proper role within the Church.

10

A Time of Disillusionment

After his conversion, Newman spent some time in England being introduced to the English Catholic community, and he, in his turn, getting to know them. In September of 1846 he went to Rome to prepare for reception of Holy Orders.[1] He was at this time rather overawed by the spectacle of Rome in operation and gave his feelings full liberty to roam. However, he still sees the supremacy of the pope in the light of the Church's faith, as witnessed by the following lines penned to his friend H. Wilberforce after his conversion:

> If the Roman Church be the Church, I take it whatever it is— and if I find that Papal Supremacy is a point of faith in it, this point of faith is not to my imagination so strange, to my reason so incredible, to my historical knowledge so utterly without evidence, as to warrant me in saying 'I *cannot* take it of faith'.[2]

Newman, though convinced of the supremacy of the pope, bases this conviction finally on the received witness and faith of the Church; as a member of this communion, he accepts whatever this community maintains as its faith. Augustine's *securus judicat orbis terrarum* is still very much at work for him.

But already at this early stage of his life in the Catholic Church, Newman was experiencing that misunderstanding from the side of authority which was to plague him the rest of his life. In early 1847 he wrote to his friend Dalgairns, a fellow convert and studying at the time in France, of his difficulties in doing what he thought to be his duty:

> It seems hard, since nations now converse by printing, not in the schools, that an English Catholic cannot investigate truth with

1. *Ward* I, pp. 162–3.
2. *Ibid.*, p. 621.

one of France or Rome without having the Inquisition upon him. What I say is, 'I am not maintaining what I say is all true, but I wish to *assist in investigating* and bringing to light *great* principles necessary for the day—*and the only way to bring these out is *freely* to investigate, with the inward habitual intention (which I trust I have) always to be submitting what I say to the judgment of the Church.[3]

This letter is quite self-explanatory. Newman haṣ met for the first time with that attitude of caution and mistrust which was to follow him for years; caution, because no one in Rome understood him; mistrust, because he was a convert. But he had come to Rome with the hope of being allowed to place all his great and proven talents to use in the cause of the Catholic Church. To be put on ice was absolutely the last thing he desired. Nevertheless, it was to happen.

In May of 1847 Newman was ordained; by the end of the year he was back in England, decided upon the Oratory as a suitable place for him within the pale of the English Catholic community.[4] It is during this period that Newman began to rebound from the almost romantic enthusiasm which had characterized his first days after his conversion. He felt that his theory of the *via media* had not collapsed because it was a bad theory; rather, he felt that it had 'broken down under *facts, historical facts*'.[5] And it was these facts, coupled with his own disillusionment as the years went by, which helped him bring a balance once more into his thought on the Church's teaching function.

In 1849, in a letter to a convert from the English Church who had become a nun, he enters into some of these historical facts, but is careful to balance them in their perspective. He begins with a discussion of Gregory the Great's supposed 'disclaimer of universal jurisdiction'. Newman does not see it that way. 'He does not disclaim it—but he disclaims being *the Bishop* of each diocese.'[6]

Newman was quite astonished, as he says, at the actual power possessed by a bishop in his diocese; even though papal power has never been greater, it is remarkable, for someone standing outside, to realize the place of a bishop in his diocese.[7] Anticipating a problem

3. *Ibid.,* p. 173 [*Newman often began a quotation or rhetorical statement with a quotation-mark and ended it with a dash, as here].
4. *Ibid.,* p. 184.
5. *Ibid.,* p. 627.
6. *Letters and Diaries* XIII, p. 283.
7. *Ibid.*

that would arise with the end of Vatican I (and which formed a guiding thought at Vatican II), Newman continues: 'Now what Pope Gregory disclaims is, his taking on himself a Bishop's jurisdiction . . . or superseding the Episcopacy, which is a very different thing from saying that he has not himself a jurisdiction over them.'[8] He distinguished here between the jurisdiction enjoyed by a bishop in his diocese and that exercised by the pope as pope. It is an important distinction, not so much for Newman's personal theology—he had always felt the power wielded by his ordinary, even in the Anglican Church[9]—but as a marker indicating the direction of his thought.

Along with pointing out the place of bishops in relationship to the pope's supremacy,[10] the problem occasioned by Augustine's famous phrase—*securus judicat orbis terrarum*—comes up once more. In light of these words, so instrumental, as we saw, in changing Newman's conception of the Church's teaching function, he can categorize all who sin against this *regula* as heretics: 'Those who contradict opinions *every where received* are heretics.'[11] He then continues, describing the situation of the Donatist heresy, and posing the question, why Augustine had called upon the authority of the universal Church, instead of that of the pope, in order to put down the claims of the heretics; it was, he maintains, a matter of fact, and as such 'the universal Church determined better than the narrow investigation of a few Bishops, or the prima facie judgment of the Holy See. As if he said, "The Pope will not be able to go against the world on this point".'[12] Again, we have Newman's conviction that it was only together—the pope determining, the universal Church witnessing—that the teaching function of the Church could be fully and properly activized.[13]

8. *Ibid.*

9. Recall his remarkable attitude during the crisis of Tract 90.

10. See F. Willam, 'Newman vor 1871 über Primat und Episkopat' in *Orientierung* 27 (1963) pp. 162–4.

11. *Letters and Diaries* XIII, p. 282.

12. *Ibid.*, p. 283.

13. In a letter written a few days after the one cited above, Newman mentions his feeling that the infallibility of the pope is to be 'looked on as a *doctrine* to be received on faith . . . by those who are to enter the Church on *other* grounds . . .'. This points out his feeling, which was to cause him so much anguish at the time of Vatican I, that papal infallibility, though for him personally no problem, should remain a matter to be received on faith in the Church, i.e. *fides ecclesiastica*, and not as a necessary condition for salvation, i.e. as a dogma; see J. Fenton, 'Newman and Papal Infallibility' in *American Essays for the Newman Centenial*, Washington, 1947, p. 167.

The second matter which will concern us here is Newman's disheartening project of the Catholic University in Ireland.[14] The whole extremely complicated history of this ill-fated attempt to found a Catholic university in Ireland which would have cared for the educational wants of the Catholics in the British Isles is not in order here; we will give a sketch of its proceedings and then bring out Newman's attitude as it is bent before the winds of opposition.

Already in 1850 Newman had seen the important role the laity would be playing in the Church of the future and was 'sure they may be made in this day the strength of the Church'.[15] If this was to be done, however, the laity would have to be equipped with the first-class education necessary for such a responsible position in today's developing pluralistic world. But first, the belief in Christianity, necessary as a basis for the laity's activity in the world, would have to be strengthened. 'The gradual spread of a secularist intellectual atmosphere did, as a matter of fact, help to destroy effectual belief in Christianity', says Ward, in describing the situation at this time.[16]

In step with this thought, Newman wanted to form, by way of a Catholic university in the British Isles, 'a body of educated and thoughtful opinion among Catholic laity' which would then take part in the movement, already in motion on the continent, to stem the tide of infidelity.[17] He wanted to equip this laity for more responsible work, a laity 'gravely and solidly educated in Catholic knowledge and alive to the arguments in its behalf, and aware both of its difficulties and of the way of treating them'.[18] It was in this atmosphere that, in April of 1851, Newman was invited to become the first rector of the Catholic University of Ireland.[19]

In order to prepare for his opening tasks, Newman began to compose addresses for delivery as introductory lectures at the inauguration of the university. These later became his *Idea of a University*, together with various other lectures delivered between 1854 and 1858. These lectures are a source for determining the state of Newman's mind during this period of his life. But even

14. The best account is still that to be found in *Ward* I, pp. 305–89.
15. *Ward* I, p. 259.
16. *Ibid.*, p. 309.
17. *Ibid.*, p. 314.
18. *Ibid.*, p. 315.
19. *Ibid.*, p. 305.

more instructive is a look into his correspondence, which arose in reaction to the situation around him.

The university had first been proposed as an answer to the rejection, by the Congregation for the Propagation of the Faith, of the Queen's College in Dublin. This rejection having been backed by the Irish episcopacy, they decided to found a university of their own, and Rome concurred. The committee set up to handle this proposal was headed by Archbishop Cullen. He it was who extended the invitation to Newman to assume the post of rector of the university.

From the first it was clear that Newman was being treated more as a figure-head than as a true rector. Appointments were made over his head; he was left sitting for confirmation of his acceptance; nothing was provided him in the way of instruments in running his organization; he was overruled in decisions he felt to be his alone by virtue of his office. Above all he met with resistance in setting his ideas into action as to what the university should be. As we have seen, he felt it to exist for the purpose of forming a cultivated and educated laity, ready to take their place in the arena of the world, ready to defend their Christianity against the unbelief of the moment.

The bishops, however, viewed the matter in another light. The university was for them a means of controlling the thought of what they felt to be already a rather rambunctious laity. They had their symbol, in the university, to set off against the Queen's Colleges, and for them that was enough. Newman immediately felt the strain of this tension-filled predicament. He felt that something great could come of this experiment, something aimed towards marshalling the full resources of the Church against the infidelity of a world gone mad in admiration of scientific processes as the answer to all possible problems. He attempted to place laymen on the faculty, and did succeed in gaining admission for a few; in general, however, the bishops opposed him every inch of the way. There was contriving going on behind his back; decisions he had made were strangely ignored.

In this atmosphere, it is no wonder that Newman's spirits began to deflate. But he kept trying to bring his ideas into harmony with those of authority: 'Nothing great or living can be done except when men are self-governed and independent; this is quite consistent with a full maintenance of ecclesiastical supremacy.'[20] He

20. *Ibid.*, I, p. 367.

truly felt that something great and good could come of giving the laity a role in the life of the Church; and he felt this could—nay, must—be done *together* with the ecclesiastical powers. He felt, after studying the great schools of the Middle Ages, that they had been precisely the arenas of free discussion so vitally necessary for the maintenance of free thought; such a freedom of thought, he felt, was just as essential for a satisfying and healthy theology as the principle of authority which controlled it and kept it from excesses.[21] This was precisely what he was trying to do in the Irish University: to maintain his conviction of the necessity of harmony between the witnessing Church—represented here by the university forum—and its determining and controlling authority—represented by the episcopacy and the Roman curia; but he was foiled at every turn.

Ward sums up Newman's views:

> In controlling Liberalism the antidote was the controlling action of the Catholic Church in arresting speculation when it ran to excesses beyond the power of man's mental digestion. Newman recognized the necessity *in its place* of free discussion. Each principle needed assertion; neither could be allowed to be supreme.[22]

But one side, at least in this instance, of this delicate balance was attempting to play the role of the supreme arbiter; supreme, in the sense that the other partner on the tandem was not allowed to perform his function.

Newman's enthusiasm waned considerably as the project of the Irish University neared its inevitable end. And yet, battling, as we have seen, for the right to expression of the whole Church in its genuine witness to its faith, he still held confidence in the very authority which was stifling that attempt. In his opening lecture, in 1852, he invokes this very authority as confidence enough to begin what would seem to be a hopeless endeavor:

> In the midst of our difficulties I have one ground of hope, just one stay, but, as I think, a sufficient one, which serves me in the stead of all other argument whatever, which hardens me against criticism, which supports me if I begin to despond, and to which I ever come round, when the question of the possible and the

21. *Ibid.,* p. 398.
22. *Ibid.,* p. 413.

expedient is brought into discussion. It is the decision of the Holy See; St. Peter has spoken, it is he who has enjoined that which seems to us so unpromising. He has spoken, and has a claim on us to trust him . . . If ever there was a power on earth who had an eye for the times, who has confined himself to the practicable, and has been happy in his anticipations, whose words have been facts, and whose commands prophecies, such is he in the history of ages, who sits from generation to generation in the Chair of the Apostles, as the Vicar of Christ, and the Doctor of His Church . . . All those who take part with the Apostle, are on the winning side.[23]

One can see the despondency on the one hand, the rock-solid confidence on the other, with which Newman wrote the above words. He had been warned, before the project even started, that its hopes for success were slim. But he embarked anyway. He had staked his all upon the chair of Peter and he would carry through. His early enthusiasm, carried over from his conversion, is here in evidence. Not just in matters of doctrine is the pope to be trusted implicitly; also in things 'practicable' is he the undeniable leader. And yet the whole wonderful project ground to a halt; and this because the authorities had failed him. Newman was hurt and it was a hurt from which he would be long in recovering.

Ward characterized the above words of Newman as 'full of pathos';[24] but Newman did not have only words of such a sort to bring out his thought on the papacy. Further along in the same lecture,[25] he emphasizes the commanding position of the pope:

Deeply do I feel, ever will I protest, *for I can appeal to the ample testimony of history to bear me out,* that in questions of right and wrong, there is nothing really strong in the whole world, nothing decisive and operative, but the voice of Him, to whom have been committed the Keys of the Kingdom, and the oversight of Christ's flock. That voice is now, as ever it has been, a real authority, *infallible* when it teaches, prosperous when it commands, ever taking the lead wisely and distinctly in its own

23. *The Idea of a University*, p. 13.
24. *Ward* I, p. 313.
25. Interestingly enough, Newman omitted the following passage in the final published version of his *Idea of a University* when he brought it out in 1859; see *Ward* I, p. 559; the citation is according to the letter, written in 1872, in which Newman pointed out that he had held the infallibility of the pope long before the decrees of Vatican I; to be found in *Ward* I, pp. 558–9.

province, adding certainty to what is probable, and persuasion to what is certain. Before it speaks, the most saintly may mistake; and after it has spoken, the most gifted must obey . . .[26]

Newman emphatically declares his conviction that the papacy is infallible, but only when it teaches; not so in its other activities, but, of course, to be obeyed with respect. That it was not infallible in its practical judgments Newman had his present experience for proof. Despite this, however, he was committed to an infallible Church with an infallible pope; the heritage of half his life spent in the English Church, searching for this source of authority, could not be wiped out. But something was missing; that something was the responsible witness of the whole Church to its faith as determined by that authority. With the question of the laity's role in the determination of church doctrine, Newman came face to face with this problem.

26. *Ward* I, pp. 558–9.

The Rambler Article

In 1859 Newman wrote an article, entitled 'On Consulting the Faithful in Matters of Doctrine',[1] for the July issue of the *Rambler,* a somewhat liberal Catholic magazine in the hands of laymen. It created an immediate storm and left its author with a cloud over his head which was not to disappear until he had been created a cardinal by Leo XIII.[2] The story is, at best, chaotic, and what really concerns us here is what Newman wrote; but why he wrote it and what occurred upon his writing it is essential enough for understanding it, that a short sketch of this affair may not be out of order as an accompaniment to Newman's thought.

The *Rambler* had been founded in 1848 by J. M. Capes, an Oxford convert; by 1858 he had been joined by Richard Simpson, a clergyman convert from Oxford, and the young Sir John Acton, who had joined the editorial staff in 1857 at the age of twenty-three.[3] 'Its aim was to re-habilitate Catholic thought in a non-Catholic world'; it did this by combining a level of scholarship, which up to that time had not been seen in Catholic periodicals, with 'attitudes critical of ecclesiastical authority which had become equally uncustomary'.[4] Newman's engagement with it began in

1. Original in the *Rambler,* July 1859, pp. 198–230; edited and republished by J. Coulson with an excellent introduction as *On Consulting the Faithful in Matters of Doctrine,* London, 1961; all citations will be according to this edition. The best account of the matter until the past few years had been Ward's telling in his biography, but Coulson's introduction has now taken its place as the most succinct and organized account of a remarkably complicated affair. See also J. Guitton, *Mitbürgern der Wahrheit,* Salzburg, 1964; it also includes the text of Newman's article. Guitton's work has appeared in English translation as *The Church and the Laity,* New York, 1965.
2. *Ward* II, p. 452.
3. *Consult. Faith.,* p. 2; see also J. L. Altholz, *The Liberal Catholic Movement in England: The 'Rambler' and its Contributors,* London, 1962, for an informative account of the stormy life of the little magazine.
4. *Consult. Faith.,* p. 2.

1859; due to the magazine's attitude, it would be hard indeed for it to escape censure in the pastorals due from the English hierarchy at Easter.[5] Newman seemed a logical choice to mediate the dispute, as both trusted by his ordinary, Bishop Ullathorne, and respected by the editors of the *Rambler*.[6]

He first of all recommended that the *Rambler* expressly stop handling theological topics.[7] But this step, even if it had been undertaken by Simpson (Acton had already left the country ahead of the impending storm[8]), would hardly have placated the bishops; they wanted someone's head to roll. By the middle of February Ullathorne wrote to Newman that the opinions of himself, Bishop Grant, Archbishop Errington and Cardinal Wiseman 'were unanimous that something must be done . . . It is our opinion that nothing short of Mr. Simpson's retiring from the Editorship will satisfy.'[9]

Simpson got wind of this development and offered to resign, but only if allowed to choose his successor; otherwise he would make a public statement as to why he was being forced out of the editorship, and he would demand redress from the bishops through the courts.[10] Of course the problem was not that simple; a successor had to be found who would be acceptable both to Simpson and to the bishops. Newman again seemed the logical choice, but he wanted no part of it. 'If there is one thing more than another I desire', he wrote to Ward on 3 March, 'it is to answer in the negative.'[11] But there was no way out if the *Rambler* was to be saved, and Newman wanted that.[12] He accepted; Simpson put

5. *Ibid.*, p. 3.
6. There seem to be several versions as to why the periodical incurred the bishops' wrath at this particular moment. Suffice it to say that both Acton and Simpson played a role with their injudicious remarks; according to Acton, in a letter to Simpson, Newman felt the action to have been provoked by 'the hope of breaking down' the *Rambler* and 'by jealousy of Doellinger' who had recently contributed to the magazine: see *Consult. Faith.*, p. 5.
7. 'I certainly think the *Rambler* is in a false position, and I have long thought so . . . I think it has been a mistake to take up theology at all . . . While it is theological, it provokes opposition, which is always practically, and becomes actually and avowedly, a siding with the Parties which the *Rambler* is opposing. Thus those parties have Catholic society with them, which naturally sides with authority.' Newman to Acton, 31 December 1858, in *Orat.*, vol. 33.
8. *Consult. Faith.*, p. 5.
9. Ullathorne to Newman, 16 February 1859, in *Orat.*, vol. 33.
10. Simpson to Ullathorne, 19 February 1859, *ibid.*
11. Newman to Ward, 3 March 1859, *ibid.*
12. Newman to Simpson, 16 March 1859, *ibid.*

the magazine into his hands at the bishop's request. But then, his object gained, Newman queries Ward: '. . . but what am I to do with the Rambler, now that I have got it?'[13] A good question: Especially since Newman obviously did not relish his new position.[14] He soon found, however, quite enough to keep him busy.

In the May issue of the magazine, buried away in a column on contemporary events, was a remark which immediately drew criticism. Unsigned, but written by Newman in his capacity as editor,[15] it dealt with the commission set up by the bishops to study the proposed action by the government on education. Newman had said: 'We do unfeignedly believe . . . that their Lordshops really desire to know the opinion of the laity on subjects in which the laity are especially concerned. If even in the preparation of a dogmatic definition the faithful are consulted, it is at least as natural to anticipate such an act of kind feeling and sympathy in great practical questions.'[16] John Gillow, professor of theology at Ushaw, immediately jumped on the word 'consult' and fired off a letter of protest.[17] In part he said: 'As a matter of principle, it seems to imply that the infallibility of the Church resides in *communitate fidelium,* and not exclusively in the *Ecclesia docenti.* Else the infallible portion would consult the fallible with a view to guiding itself to an infallible decision.'

Newman's answer contains what in the long run would prove to be the decisive view, though at the time it certainly did not carry the day. He pointed out that if the passage had been in Latin, then the word 'consult' should not have been used. Newman felt, however, that 'in popular English it seems to me neither inaccurate nor dangerous . . . In this sense of the word—ascertaining a fact—surely the *sensus fidelium* has a real place in the evidences (*per modum unius*) of apostolical tradition and in the preliminaries of a dogmatic definition.'[18] Newman goes on to quote Perrone, whom he had seen and talked to in Rome in 1846–47, and who supported this view in his own dogmatic. Gillow wrote back in complete

13. Newman to Ward, 10 March 1859, *ibid.*
14. In a letter to Ullathorne on 23 March, Newman characterized it as a 'most bitter penance'; in *Orat.,* vol. 33.
15. *Consult. Faith.,* p. 8.
16. *Ibid.*
17. 12 May 1859, in *Orat.,* vol. 34.
18. Newman to Gillow, 16 May 1859, *ibid.*

agreement with Newman's explanation, but still objecting to the use of the word 'consult'.[19]

In the meantime Ullathorne had called on Newman to talk of the *Rambler*; in the course of his conversation with Newman he said: 'Our laity are a *peaceable* set; the Church is *peace*. They have a deep faith; they do not like to hear that anyone doubts . . . he said something like, "who are the laity?" I answered (not these *words*) that the Church would look foolish without them.' He went on to ask Newman to surrender the editorship of the *Rambler* and Newman said he would after the July issue.[20]

Here, in all its pregnant fullness, is Newman's thought on the participation of the laity as guaranteed by the role played in the teaching function of the Church by the *whole* Church in its character as witnessing to its faith. It does not deny the active character assigned to the *ecclesia docens*; on the contrary, it brings out in great clarity the cooperation essential for the full development of each in its respective role. It is a *whole* Church Newman is talking about, not one split into two separate camps. The teaching office 'ascertains' the fact of the whole Church's witness; on the basis of this witness, in which it itself is a co-witness, it determines the validity of the witness and its extent.

In the bishop's answer one can see all too clearly the attitude which made Newman's efforts always seem so futile. It has always been this way, and if it continues so, there will be peace; but in any case the boat was not to be rocked. The laity were to be kept in their places, thus making the place of both the laity and of authority secure as they were.

Gillow, in the meantime, kept up his attack on the word 'consult'. Newman tried repeatedly to make it clear to him that a distinction was necessary if one were to understand his meaning properly; but to no avail. He finally felt driven to author an article in defense of his choice of words; this was the famous 'On Consulting the Faithful in Matters of Doctrine'. It was the last issue appearing under his guidance, and he felt he was now done with the matter. But hardly had the magazine reached its readers than Gillow was back at the pen again, complaining that the defense of the word 'consult' was not at all successful, and that a claim advanced in the article—that the body of bishops during the Arian heresy had been

19. Gillow to Newman, 18 May 1859, *ibid.*
20. A memorandum of Newman's dated 22 May 1859, *ibid.*

suspended in their office as the *ecclesia docens*—was highly irregular, to say the least. Newman tried to make it clear to him that an important distinction was necessary if one were to understand his meaning: 'You consider "suspense" in the article to mean "failure"; I think it has a meaning far lighter than "suspension". You consider that "the body of the Bishops" in the article means the *"Ecclesia docens"*: I think it merely means the actual mass at the particular time spoken of.'[21]

This was Newman's point, and he had history on his side. But Gillow proved adamant. He alerted Bishop Brown of Newport concerning the whole affair. Brown, in turn, deleted the article to Rome, without, however, informing Newman of his action.[22] A month later Talbot is able to write to Ullathorne that the article had raised a commotion in Rome and perhaps if Newman knew this he would be more careful in the future: 'he has lost the confidence of many in consequence of it, and the Rambler is beginning to be looked upon as a very dangerous periodical.'[23] And thus a cloud formed over Newman, not to leave him for twenty years.

Through an almost unbelievable series of blunders on the side of Newman's ordinary, Ullathorne, and his metropolitan, Wiseman, the opportunity to reply to the charges made against him was being taken out of his hands. But what is it he said that raised such a storm?

In fact, Newman was maintaining nothing more than what he had held ever since his *Arians of the Fourth Century*. But as a Catholic, his choice of language, as he himself admitted,[24] could have been more prudent. For him it was 'a matter of fact' about which the faithful were to be consulted; they were not to be asked their opinion, but 'their belief, *is* sought for, as a testimony to that apostolical tradition, on which alone any doctrine whatsoever can

---

21. Newman to Gillow, 28 August 1859, *ibid.*
22. Brown's letter—a photostat is in *Orat.*, vol. ·35—is to be found in the original in *Scrip. Ref. Anglia,* vol. 15, f. 1080, of the Cong. Prop. Fide in Rome; it is dated 3 October 1859 and charges that 'there are propositions . . . which appear to me totally subversive of the essential authority of the Church in matters of faith'. In a later letter to Monsignor Talbot in Rome he admonishes him to call 'the attention of His Holiness to the positive heresy brought out under the editorship of Newman, or rather (for it is I believe the fact) coming from his pen': Brown to Talbot, 7 October 1859, in *Orat.*, vol. 35.
23. Talbot to Ullathorne, 3 December 1859, in *Orat., vol.* 35.
24. *Ward* II, p. 125.

be defined . . . they are witnesses to the antiquity or universality of the doctrines . . . about which they are "consulted" '.[25]

Here is Newman's thought in its finest hour. In this short statement he has given the essence of his thought over the past forty years. We have followed it through all its detours and side paths; it is now on the track of the balance he had found to play such an important role in the Arian conflict. He continues with a discussion of *why* the faithful are consulted for their witness: 'because the body of the faithful is one of the witnesses to the fact of the tradition of revealed doctrine, and because their *consensus* through Christendom is the voice of the Infallible Church.'[26]

In line with this, Newman contends that the tradition of the Apostles was committed to the *whole* Church and it manifests itself 'in its various constituents and functions *per modum unius*'.[27] At the same time he grants that 'the gift for discerning, discriminating, defining, promulgating, and enforcing any portion of that tradition resides solely in the *Ecclesia docens*'.[28]

Thus it is *one* Church which teaches; the one Church determining through its witness; the one Church determining that witness; it is one Church functioning in its twofold aspect. Newman emphasizes this when he cites the definition, in 1854, of the Immaculate Conception; in the pope's bull of definition 'the two, the Church teaching and the Church taught, are put together, as one twofold testimony, illustrating each other, and never to be divided'.[29] He would spend the rest of his theological career trying to keep those two aspects of the teaching function of the Church together.

The other statement which caused so much furor concerned a historical fact. During the Arian controversy, said Newman, 'the divine dogma of our Lord's divinity was proclaimed, enforced, maintained, and (humanly speaking) preserved, far more by the "Ecclesia docta" than by the "Ecclesia docens" . . . the body of the episcopate was unfaithful to its commission, while the body of the laity was faithful to its baptism . . . there was a temporary suspense of the functions of the "Ecclesia docens". The body of the Bishops failed in their confession of the faith.'[30]

25. *Consult. Faith.*, p. 55.
26. *Ibid.*, p. 63.
27. *Ibid.*
28. *Ibid.*
29. *Ibid.*, p. 71.
30. *Ibid.*, pp. 76–7.

For Newman this was a fact of history; and he had no difficulty in showing that his facts were accurate. Besides:

> There could be no real failure of the *Ecclesia docens* while the decree of Nicaea against Arianism remained the official expression of its ruling on the side of orthodoxy . . . he had not maintained . . . that even after the Council the *coetus episcoporum* in its corporate capacity was heretical, but that Bishops as individuals failed to vindicate the orthodox doctrine. The fact that the bulk of the Bishops were for a time individually disloyal to the official teaching of their own body was no more a denial of the infallibility of the *Ecclesia docens* than the fact that a Pope might personally hold an unorthodox opinion would be a denial of the infallibility of his *ex cathedra* definitions.[31]

For Newman, '. . . each constituent portion of the Church has its proper functions, and no portion can safely be neglected'.[32]

The Church was a communion 'with a common conscience, that of all its members, and was not to be looked on as a mere juridical entity, ruled by officers'. This teaching, 'which was to be incorporated in the Conciliar Decree on the Church at the Second Vatican Council, was resented among the English Catholic authorities and theologians, but no one was in a position to dispute Newman's fact'.[33] Perhaps English theologians did not appreciate this thought, but the Roman Franzelin took up the question as posed and attempted to give it an objective critique.[34] It was not

31. *Ward* I, pp. 503–4; see also a memorandum, drawn up by Newman as a possible answer to the charges brought against him in Rome, dated 21 January 1860, in *Orat.*, vol. 36. He explains that he used the word 'body' in the phrase 'body of bishops' in a material sense, not *in se*: *Jam vero dixit anonymus Episcopi materialiter accepti defuerunt in confessione sua. Materies, non corpus Anglice 'body' non habet distinctum illud et definitum quod theologiae verba habent. Vult aliquando 'corpus' i.e. ut formatum, aliquando 'materies' ut cum dicimus 'vinum habet body' i.e. solidam, bonam, plenam materiem. Hic non vult 'corpus', quia loquitur anonymus de 'body laicorum', sed laici non constituunt per se corpus formale, sed materiem quandam quae una cum hierarchia facit unum corpus.* This should certainly suffice in clearing the matter.

32. *Consult. Faith.*, p. 103.

33. C. S. Dessain, *John Henry Newman*, London, 1967, p. 116; see also O. Karrer, in the introduction to his translation of Newman's 'On Consulting the Faithful', in *Hochland* 40 (1947/48) 402.

34. See his *Tractatus de divina traditione et scriptura*, 1870¹, pp. 94–104; 1882³, pp. 103–14. Newman answered him in his third edition of *The Arians of the Fourth Century*, p. 467. See also M. Scheeben, as quoted in W. Bartz, *Die lehrende Kirche*, Trier, 1959, for an astounding similarity in views: pp. 67, 148, 151, and p. 70, footnote 146.

the first time,[35] nor would it be the last,[36] that Newman would voice his feelings on this fundamental problem. But his thought was cast now, and it remained for him to define it more sharply in its relationship to the specific problem of papal infallibility in the storms which were beginning to rise around Vatican I.

35. See especially *Hist. Sketch.* I, pp. 209–10, for an impressive statement on how the body of the faithful has transmitted the faith, through its witness, down through the centuries.
36. See Appendix, p. 136, below.

12

The Apologia

The incident which called forth Newman's volcanic reaction—his *Apologia pro vita sua*—need not detain us here.[1] It will suffice for our study if we observe that Part VI of the first edition (it is Part V of the second edition) was written in answer to a request of Acton's, namely that Newman take up the recent condemnation handed down by Pius IX on the so-called 'Munich Conference'.

In August 1863, Döllinger, Alzog and Abbot Haneburg invited a large number of Catholic scholars to the Benedictine monastery in Munich for a conference.[2] The pope telegraphed his blessings. The archbishop of Bamberg and the bishop of Augsburg were there and gave several toasts. Döllinger delivered a keynote address with a ringing cry for a theology more suited to modern needs than the scholastic system, despite the advances won by the latter. Faithfulness to truth and recognition of the development of thought forms were the major ideas. Heinrich and Scheeben, two of Germany's most outstanding theologians, were present and did not openly disagree. But suddenly, on 21 December 1863, Pius IX came down hard on the conference;[3] the results were far-reaching.

Infallibility now became a burning topic.[4] People saw in Pius IX's condemnation the proof that the Church, 'so far from being truth's champion . . . appeared to subordinate Revelation to the *ipse dixit* of its own infallibility'.[5] One further consequence of this action was that Lord Acton, feeling that in the light of the Munich Brief he could not continue in his work, brought the *Home and*

---

1. See *Ward* II, pp. 1–46, for an excellent account of the challenge and Newman's writing of the *Apologia*.
2. See *Ward* I, pp. 562ff; the rest of the account given is taken from Ward.
3. The famous 'Munich Brief' in: AAS 8 (1874) 438ff, as *Tuas libenter*; excerpts are in Denzinger[31], §§ 1679–1684.
4. C. S. Dessain, *J. H. Newman*, p. 124.
5. *Ibid.*

Foreign Review to an end. It had been the successor to the *Rambler* and despite its sometimes rather imprudent language, had played an important role in the Catholic community of England.

On 10 April 1864 Acton wrote to Newman saying that if Newman were to reply to the charges from Kingsley on his being a teacher of untruth, he should also 'widen the scope of his reply to go into some of the questions in which the *Home and Foreign Review* had been involved'.[6] He also urged Newman to 'enlighten not only the Protestants but such Catholics as have got a little confused by the policy which is adopted in order to avoid scandal'; he should also deal 'with the difficulty which many seem to feel in the practice of proscribing truth and positively encouraging falsehood in the Church'.[7] Newman replied to Acton that 'as to the points you mention, you may be sure I shall go as far as ever I can'.[8] The result of this attempt was the first half of Part VII of the *Apologia* in its first edition, on the 'Position of my Mind since 1845'. 'There Newman on the one hand defended and showed the limits of the Church's infallibility, and on the other, protested against authoritarianism.'[9]

We must remember, too, that Newman's statements on infallibility were 'intended to be . . . not a declaration of minimism, but a plain statement of the belief obligatory upon Catholics at that time, i.e. six years before the Vatican definition'.[10] This is important. Newman, though never having any trouble accepting papal infallibility himself, felt that it would be an unnecessary hardship for many people to demand belief in that doctrine as if it were a declared dogma. Until the definition of Vatican I, as we shall see, Newman always felt it better to consider it a theological opinion, rather than a binding dogma.[11]

Therefore, as to the *Apologia*, 'it must be recollected that it was not a didactic work—nor did it contain a statement of my own personal views about infallibility, but was addressed to Protestants *in order to show* them what it was that a Catholic fairly undertook in the way of theological profession when he becomes a Catholic'.[12]

6. *Ibid.*, p. 125.
7. *Ibid.*
8. *Ibid.*
9. *Ibid.*
10. H. Tristram, *Cardinal Newman's Papers on Infallibility, 1866–68*, typed, compiled and edited with an introduction by Tristram in *Orat.*, B.7.4., 1.
11. *Flanagan*, p. 591.
12. *Ibid.*

Thus in the first edition[13] Newman cited 'two or three sentences from Chrismann which professed less about the province of Infallibility than I held myself'.[14] Newman withdrew these two sentences in the second edition[15] 'because they seemed too strong an *assertion* and to be taking a side,—whereas I wished to be vague'. He wished so, because he felt that his task was to 'correctly exhibit and represent the current opinion'; not to put forth his own opinion, which, though it might be true, nevertheless 'might perplex and unsettle those having no difficulties'. 'I cannot', he goes on, 'bear tyrant majorities, and I am tender about minorities, but I have no wish that minorities should kick up their heels, and throw the majority into confusion.'[16]

Beside the Munich Brief, another cause which brought Newman to discuss infallibility in his *Apologia* was the exaggeration being laid upon this office of the pope by W. G. Ward, Archbishop Manning and the school of the *Univers* in France.[17] Newman felt that he at last had a chance to defend his analysis of the problematic, which fell far short of that represented by those named above. 'He felt that these more extreme writers overlooked historical facts and theological distinctions.'[18] Afterwards he could write to Pusey that '. . . I so dislike Ward's way of going on, that I can't get myself to read the *Dublin*. But on those points I have said my say in my "Apologia" . . . But, while I would maintain my own theological opinions, I don't dispute Ward the right of holding his, so long that he does not attempt to impose them on me.'[19]

Two months later he is back on the subject again:

> As to the Infallibility of the Pope, I see nothing against it, or to dread in it,—for I am confident that it *must* be so limited practically that it will leave things as they are. As to Ward's notions,

13. *Apol.,* 1st edition, p. 329.
14. *Flanagan,* p. 592. P. N. Chrismann, a German Franciscan, had published in 1792 a work, *Regula Fidei Catholicae et Collectio Dogmatum Credendorum;* it was republished (Würzburg 1854) by Spindler, a student of Döllinger's. The sentences Newman used were: I. *Ecclesia non gaudet infallibiliter assistentia Spiritus S. in docendis recte veritatibus, quae ratione tantum ex revelatis, licet evidenter, concluduntur;* II. *Judicium Ecclesiae non est infallibile, quando homines damnat, tanquam haereticos, qui falsam doctrinam tradiderunt* (pp. 95–6).
15. *Apol.,* 2nd edition, p. 253.
16. *Flanagan,* pp. 592–3.
17. *Ward* II, p. 36.
18. *Ibid.*
19. *Ibid.,* pp. 91–2.

they are preposterous,—nor do I see anything in the Pope's Encyclical [i.e. the Syllabus of Pius IX] to confirm them . . . nothing comes from the Pope without having weight, but there is a great difference between weight and infallibility.[20]

In the light of these remarks, the section Newman dedicated in his *Apologia* to the problematic of papal infallibility takes on added importance; in it he 'indicates the functions of authority in the formation of Catholic theology'.[21] How, then, did he treat it?

Newman begins with what he calls the 'preamble' to the Church's teaching task: the anarchical situation in which man finds himself: in 'this living busy world', there is 'no reflection of its Creator'.[22] For Newman this is an empirical fact; it is an experience he makes when observing the world and man's place within it. This fact constitutes 'one of those great difficulties of this absolute primary truth', i.e. of the being of God.[23] These two facts, man's real situation in the world and the being of God, are so incongruous and incommensurate, that Newman must search for an explanation. His only answer is 'that either there is no Creator, or this living society of men is in a true sense discarded from His presence'.[24] He opts for the second possibility: '*if* there be a God, *since* there is a God, the human race is implicated in some terrible aboriginal calamity.'[25] This Newman calls original sin.[26]

Given this background, Newman then supposes what this Creator would do if he wanted to interfere in this chaotic condition of mankind; what would the methods be, if he were to attempt to set things aright once more? Newman sees one antagonist to such an effort on the part of man's Creator; that is the 'all-corroding, all-dissolving scepticism of the intellect in religious inquiries'.[27] This intellect of man's, from its nature directed towards the truth, has, in fact, and viewed actually and historically, 'the tendency towards a simple unbelief in matter of religion'.[28] How then is

20. *Ibid.*, p. 101.
21. *Ibid.*, p. 38.
22. *Apol.*, p. 241.
23. *Ibid.*
24. *Ibid.*, p. 242.
25. *Ibid.*
26. *Ibid.*, p. 243.
27. *Ibid.*
28. *Ibid.*

man's Creator, supposing he were to interfere in human affairs, to confront such a characteristic of man's intellect?

Newman reiterates that his solution is not the only possible one, but yet 'there is nothing to surprise the mind, if He should think fit to introduce a power into the world, invested with the prerogative of infallibility in religious matters'.[29] Why such a provision? Because it 'would be a direct, immediate, active, and prompt means of withstanding the difficulty; it would be an instrument suited to the need'.[30] In the light of this thought, Newman finds himself led to speak of the Church's infallibility as 'a provision, adapted by the mercy of the Creator, to preserve religion in the world, and to restrain that freedom of thought, which of course in itself is one of the greatest of our natural gifts, and to rescue it from its own suicidal excesses'.[31]

Infallibility, then, is an aspect, a most important aspect, but just an aspect, of the Church's teaching function; it is the guarantee that the Church's teaching activity will not be completely in vain; it is present in the Church in order to protect its normal and regular teaching task from the encroachments of man's reason gone wild; it is an 'emphatic protest against the existing state of mankind'.[32] Man has rebelled against his Creator; this was the initial cause for God's interference in the world; and the agent of his interference— the Church—must be empowered to proclaim his message to the world with certainty. What then, is this power?

Newman is not concerned with determining the seat of this divinely given power; nor is he here concerned with extending its jurisdiction beyond religious opinion.[33] Given these two limitations, he defines it as follows:

> It claims, when brought into exercise but in the legitimate manner, for otherwise of course it is but quiescent, to know for certain the very meaning of every portion of that Divine Message in detail, which was committed by our Lord to His Apostles. It claims to know its own limits, and to decide what it can determine absolutely and what it cannot.[34]

29. *Ibid.*, p. 245.
30. *Ibid.*
31. *Ibid.*
32. *Ibid.*, p. 246.
33. *Ibid.*, p. 249.
34. *Ibid.*, p. 250.

Three important qualifications are laid down in this definition:
1) the Church's infallibility can only be brought into action under
certain conditions, otherwise it is dormant and cannot function;
2) when these conditions are present, and this power can be acti-
vated, then it is able to determine, with a certainty that normally
escapes the human intellect in its natural functions, the exact
meaning of any part of God's revelation given in Christ to the
world; 3) this power has limits beyond which it cannot function—
and it can itself determine these limits—and knows that it cannot
act beyond them. It is a power to interpret, not to make.[35] As such,
it is but a guarantee, as Newman said above, that God's revelation,
as given to the world and entrusted to the Church, will remain
pure and unsullied; otherwise God's intervention would have
been in vain. This is a thought which Newman had already made
and partly developed in his *Prophetical Office* some twenty years
before, in speaking of the Church's indefectibility.

But what of man's reason? Is it to be stilled forever in the presence
of such a power? No, says Newman. He quotes St Paul to the
effect that Paul's apostolical power had been given him to
edification, and not to destruction:

> There can be no better account of the Infallibility of the Church.
> It is a supply for a need, and it does not go beyond that need. Its
> object is, and its effect also, not to enfeeble the freedom or
> vigour of human thought in religious speculation, but to resist
> and control its extravagance.[36]

The Church's infallibility is not the avowed enemy of man's
reason; it is but a protection, a correction, against its overflowings
and enthusiastic orgies of thought and speculation. 'Catholic
Christendom is no simple exhibition of religious absolutism, but
presents a continuous picture of Authority and Private Judgment
alternately advancing and retreating as the ebb and flow of the
tide.'[37] It is this dialectical process in the attempt to gain truth
which Newman finds absolutely 'necessary for the very life of
religion, viewed in its large operations and its history'; it is imperative that 'the warfare should be incessantly carried on'—the

35. *Ibid.*, p. 251.
36. *Ibid.*, p. 253.
37. *Ibid.*, p. 252.

warfare between authority and man's reason as expressed in private judgment.[38]

Given this situation for the exercise of infallibility, Newman lists the limitations which are set upon it. First of all, 'Infallibility cannot act outside of a definite circle of thought, and it must in all its decisions, or *definitions,* as they are called, profess to be keeping within it. The great truths of the moral law, of natural religion, and of Apostolical faith, are both its boundary and its foundation.'[39] It determines and interprets; it does not create. It is a light which illuminates the truths mankind needs in order to repair the breach between itself and its Creator. But it does not tyrannize in its own arbitrariness. It is bound to the truth, and this truth is its justification for existence. Futhermore, 'it must ever profess to be guided by Scripture and tradition'.[40] Therefore, says Newman, nothing can be presented to him to believe, as part of the faith, which he should not already have believed, and has only not been able to do so because it was not presented. And nothing can be laid upon him to believe which is 'different in kind' from what he already holds.[41]

Using the then recent definition of the Immaculate Conception as an example, Newman points out, as a general principle to be held in regard to this role of infallibility, that 'it is a simple fact to say, that Catholics have not come to believe it because it is defined, but that it was defined because they believed it'.[42] He is not saying that infallible judgments are bound up with a consensus of the Church, or that something like a vote must be taken to determine whether a doctrine is to be defined or not. He is saying much more than that. Witness and consensus are two different things. The former implies a fact—as he pointed out in his *Rambler* article— while the latter implies asking for agreement. It is on the basis of the fact of faith that infallibility—or the teaching function of the Church, of which it is but an aspect—moves into action. It is upon the witness to the faith that it determines and illuminates. It bears, itself, witness to the witnessed faith of the Church, and in the process determines with absolute certainty the extent and limits of the initial witness.

38. *Ibid.*
39. *Ibid.,* p. 253.
40. *Ibid.*
41. *Ibid.*
42. *Ibid.,* p. 255.

Newman then turns to the problem which had been raised by the Munich Brief. He views this problematic as one of the great trials for reason in its confrontation with the Church's infallibility. In his mind, the Church's teaching authority has an indirect jurisdiction over matters and areas which are beyond its proper and natural limits.[43] As he sees it, the Church could not properly defend religious truth unless it had this jurisdiction, in order to protect its own province. But when it does so act, 'it does not so much speak doctrinally, as enforce measures of discipline'.[44] It must, of course, be obeyed in these censures and disciplinary actions. But these injunctions 'are laid merely upon our actions, not upon our thoughts . . . authoritative prohibitions may tease and irritate, but they have no bearing whatever upon the exercise of reason'.[45] They are given in the wisdom of the Church, in order that those developments, which at the moment do not appear opportune, may have their hour of glory when the moment comes. 'There is a time for everything' is one of Newman's favorite thoughts, and he feels it is only prudent to wait for the proper time before going ahead.

Various persons, he says, have asked him to come forth as a champion of Catholic truth against the scepticism and rational excesses of the day, but he feels that the time is not ripe for such an undertaking; the situation is not clear enough to admit of a satisfactory answer.[46] It is a time which calls for Christian patience; it is a time which allows that the alarmed and frightened within the Christian community can be helped only by exhorting them to faith and patience.[47] Thus, 'recent acts of the Church's authority' are to be interpreted as tying the hands of controversialists and teaching them prudence and patience.[48] Obviously he refers here to *Tuas libenter* and the request from Acton that he undertake, in Döllinger's cause, an exposition of authority's excesses. Newman feels this would be entirely out of place, because the situation simply does not admit of doing justice to the entire problem. But he emphasizes that this does not forbid further thought on the matters involved; it simply calls for silence and patience at the moment.

43. *Ibid.*, p. 257.
44. *Ibid.*
45. *Ibid.*, p. 258.
46. *Ibid.*, pp. 262–3.
47. *Ibid.*, p. 263.
48. *Ibid.*

Is this hurtful to reason and thought?[49] No, says Newman; quite the contrary. No condemnation has come down; no blocking of the freedom of thought; nothing but a call to a legitimate use of reason. 'Catholicity', he says, 'is not only one of the notes of the Church, but, according to divine purposes, one of its securities.'[50] It is this very catholicity which demands consideration of the whole Church, not only from the side of authority, but from the side of the individual. Thus authority is governed in its laying down of a determination of the witness of the Church by its catholicity, and private judgment in the garb of reason is also bound by this same catholicity. It is the whole church—the *catholic* church— which protects and guards the revelation of Christ. It does this in its unceasing witness thereto, guided and shielded by the divine gift of infallibility.

49. See Appendix, p. 138, below.
50. *Apol.*, p. 269.

13

Infallibility and Vatican I

With his *Apologia,* Newman experienced a sort of rebirth as far as his public position was concerned. Yet in addressing himself to the problems of the hour, he was prone to be cautious and examine carefully the impact such an action might have. He felt that intervention in current debates would perhaps not be the wisest action on his part.[1]

Problems there were. One of the most pressing was that of the papacy. Pius IX, who had ascended the papal throne a declared friend of reform in 1846, had become, with the passage of time and the attacks upon the temporal power of the papacy, a confirmed enemy of all liberally tinged movements.[2] A group of neo-ultramontanes arose to defend the pope's position. They included Veuillot, editor of the *Univers*; W. G. Ward, Newman's ally during the last years of the Oxford Movement, and now editor of the *Dublin Review* and a man of most imprudent language; Archbishop Manning, Newman's metropolitan. This group looked for further centralization as the only way to save the pope's position. They were opposed mainly by the French hierarchy, represented by Archbishop Sibour of Paris and Bishop Dupanloup of Orleans.[3] The militant group tended to characterize everybody who did not agree with them as disloyal to the Church and to the pope. Newman's reaction was typical. In a memorandum dated 1867 he says: 'Are they not doing the Holy See a grave disservice, who will not let a zealous man defend it *in his own way,* but insist on his doing it in *their* way or not at all—or rather only at the price

1. *Ward* II, pp. 202–3.
2. *Ibid.,* p. 209.
3. *Ibid.,* pp. 209–11.

of being considered heterodox or disaffected if his opinions do not run in a groove?'[4]

To understand better the temper of this militant group, it would be well to read some of the material being published at that time in the *Univers*. In one issue they published the hymn 'Rerum Deus Tenax Vigor', but substituted the name of 'Pius' for that of 'Deus'. In another issue they printed a hymn, dedicated to Pius IX, which recalled the hymn addressed to the Holy Spirit on Pentecost:

> *Pater pauperum,*
> *Dator munerum,*
> *Lumen cordium,*
> *Emitte coelitus*
> *Lucis tuae radium.*[5]

Newman certainly did not recoil against the good in the movement. It was intended to strengthen the faithful in 'listening to the voice of the reigning Pontiff as ever witnessing to the unerring faith of Peter'.[6] As we have seen, Newman was ever on the side of obedience to authority; but he foresaw the terrible effects such exaggerations would reap in time to come. He felt that something had to be done.

In 1865–66, in his reply to Pusey, he had planned also to answer Ward as regards papal infallibility, but he gave this idea up as being out of place.[7] However, as 1867 dawned, and one of the fathers in his house, Ignatius Ryder, intended to write a pamphlet in answer to Ward, Newman saw his best way to lie in encouraging the younger man in his endeavors.[8] There were two points Newman wanted to see emphasized in Ryder's reply. One was the degree of freedom a Catholic can exercise over his internal assent to a doctrine which has not been strictly defined as an article of faith. The second was that statements of the pope are not to be interpreted by the individual, but have to be sifted and weighed in their connection with other doctrines by the whole Church, specifically by the *schola theologorum*.[9]

When Ryder's pamphlet appeared in 1867, Newman was therefore in a position to defend its various points to his friends. Writing

4. *Ibid.*, p. 208.
5. *Ibid.*, p. 212.
6. *Ibid.*, p. 214.
7. *Ibid.*, p. 215.
8. *Ibid.*
9. *Ibid.*, p. 216.

to Ward, he states that, although he had nothing to do with its composition, he does 'agree with it heartily'[10] and feels that those who think differently from Ward on this subject have a right to do so, so long as only Ward, and not the Church, considers the matter vital to the life of faith. Newman thought that the Church 'may define' papal infallibility, but felt that it would not.[11] He held firmly to the fullest extension of the pope's jurisdiction and power; but he felt such power and jurisdiction to be principles of Catholic doctrine, and not the doctrine itself.[12] The question had never carried much importance for him personally. Holding by *fides implicita* all that the Church held or was likely to hold, he saw himself as a loyal member of the Church:

> For myself I have never taken any great interest in the question of the limits and seat of infallibility. I was converted simply because the Church was to last to the end, and that no communion answered to the Church of the first ages but the Roman Communion, both in substantial likeness and in actual descent. And as to faith, my great principle was: 'Securus judicat orbis terrarum'. So I say now—and in all these questions of detail I say—to myself, I believe whatever the Church teaches as the voice of God—and this or that particular inclusively, *if* she teaches this—it is this *fides implicita* which is our comfort in these irritating times.[13]

We see Newman still clinging to his belief that it is the whole Church which teaches—and not isolated instances. His great fear was that a definition of papal infallibility would seem to give approval to the ideas of Veuillot, Ward and their associates, ideas which for Newman were at variance with Catholic tradition. He feared that an exaggeration in this area would lead to churches being erected within the one Church; for him this was nothing more than a replay of the Novatian heresy. Thus in light of the Ryder controversy and the events between 1867 and 1870, it became clear that the question was not so much that of the extent of infallibility—the acceptance on all sides of the constitution *Pastor aeternus* at the Vatican Council showed this—but a question about the functions of the Church, especially the active theological

10. *Ibid.*, p. 224.
11. *Ibid.*, p. 221.
12. *Ibid.*, p. 223.
13. *Ibid.*, p. 234.

thought in the Church, in determining precisely what was infallible and what was not.[14]

For Newman the extent of infallibility was clear; the 'subject
matter of infallibility is only that which the Oracle of infallibility
declares to be in the depositum. It is in no sense at any time a new
revelation, unless in the sense of subjective to Catholics here or
there'.[15] Thus he writes on 16 July 1866, that the infallibility of the
Church is by a 'divine *assistentia*':

> her infallibility is *referable and ministrative* to and bounded by the
> original revelation and depositum . . . The main point I wish to
> ascertain is whether I may not hold: 1) the Church's infallibility
> is *wholly* ministrative to the depositum (custos, testis, judex,
> magistra depositi). 2) that none of her assertions must be received
> under pain of damnation, except such as are declarative and
> definitive of the depositum.[16]

Newman here presents once more his balanced view of the
Church's teaching as being a witness, a whole witness, to the faith
of the Church as based upon the revelation of God in Christ. In
another memorandum he considers this again:

> 'Securus judicat orbis terrarum.' When we say that the Church
> infallibly protects herself, this means, when regarded as a whole,
> and when she does so on principle. It need not be so as regards
> particular, undeliberate, and local acts . . .[17] may not the 'securus
> judicat orbis terrarum' supply the test, subsequent to an ecclesi-
> astical decision, whether that decision is infallible or not?[18]

In other words, how is one to know whether a decision is in fact
infallible? The definition itself could carry these credentials; but
when it does not, would not the witness of the whole Church then
serve as the measure against which it is to be drawn, in order to
compare it to its original basis? And one of the major components

---

14. See R. Dibble, *J. H. Newman: The Concept of Infallible Doctrinal Authority*,
Washington, 1955. Although this is the only full study to date of Newman's
overall thought on infallibility, it should be used with great care; Dibble has a
tendency to put words into Newman's mouth, and sometimes he seriously
misreads him. In general it is not to be trusted unless thoroughly checked against
Newman's original statements.

15. *Orat.*, B.7.4, 'Newman's Papers on Infallibility'.

16. *Ibid.*, a memorandum.

17. *Ibid.*

18. *Ibid.*, dated 10 July 1866.

of the whole Church engaged in this task is the *schola theologorum*; Newman treats this more fully in his later *Letter addressed to the Duke of Norfolk*.[19] Basically he felt that it was the 'Church' which was fitted 'with the gift of knowing its true and full meaning'.[20] This is contained in the fact that the Church is like unto the Apostles, i.e. 'in her whole evolution of ages, per modum unius, a living, present treasury of the Mind of the Spirit of Christ'.[21] What is meant, however, by the mind of the Church? For 'the Church is not a person, as an Apostle is, but is merely *made up* of fathers and theologians, and how can they altogether have one mind, which is not the mind of each?'[22] Newman says that you cannot answer, it is the mind of the infallible pope; for he is not an Apostle—and thus infallible *in habitu*—but only infallible *ex cathedra*—that is, *in actu*:

> I conceive then that the Depositum is in such sense committed to the Church or to the Pope, that when the Pope sits in St. Peter's chair, or when a Council of Fathers and doctors is collected round him, it is capable of being presented to their minds with that fullness and exactness, under the operation of supernatural grace . . . with which it habitually, not occasionally resided in the minds of the Apostles . . .[23]

It was due to such thoughts as these that Newman awaited the Vatican Council and its definition with dread. If the militants were allowed their way, an exaggeration would be introduced into the Church's teaching office, an exaggeration which could only lead to an isolation, i.e. a church within a church.[24]

The First Vatican Council was formally announced on 26 June 1867.[25] In 1868 Pius IX invited Newman to take part in the preparation of the *schemata* as a *peritus,* but he declined.[26] He was conscious of defending a position contrary to that of the pope's.

---

19. See also Appendix, p. 139, below.
20. *Flanagan,* p. 595.
21. *Ibid.,* p. 594.
22. *Ibid.,* p. 595.
23. *Ibid.,* p. 596. See also Dibble, *op. cit.,* p. 289, where he transcribes this letter of Newman's falsely: *Flanagan,* p. 593, has 'Now as to the Apostles . . .', because Newman will treat here of infallibility *in habitu,* as in the Apostles; Dibble has: 'Now as to the Popes . . .', thus twisting Newman's point 180 degrees.
24. *Ward* II, p. 233.
25. *Ibid.,* p. 210.
26. *Ibid.,* p. 240; cf. *Orat.,* vol. 44, letters 4 and 6.

It was very difficult for him to decline, but he felt that in doing so he was furthering the interests of Catholic theology against extremists—against men who were pushing, secretly and with intrigue, for a definition which would express their own personal devotional beliefs, but which, without proper care, could make it unnecessarily difficult for Catholic scholars in the future, i.e. for the very men who should defend the expected definition.[27] In the face of this, Newman felt called to do all he could without making the situation worse; and it was a most delicate situation at best.

First he asked friends to take to the public and castigate the devious activity which was bordering on scandal:

> Here is the Archbishop in a Pastoral or Pamphlet putting out extreme views—getting it read to the Pope, and circulating that the Pope approved of it—all with a view of anticipating and practising upon the judgments of the Bishops, when they meet for a General Council. Of course, what the General Council speaks is the word of God—but still we may well feel indignant at the intrigue, trickery, and imperiousness which is the human side of its history—and it seems a dereliction of duty not to do one's part to meet them.[28]

In line with this we find Newman writing to the bishops and theologians he knew might have influence in Rome and pounding home one thought: 'You are going too fast, you are going too fast.'[29] At this time Dupanloup, hearing that Newman had rejected the pope's offer to come to Rome, made his own offer that Newman accompany him to Rome as his personal theologian; Newman again declined, thinking he could do more by staying home.[30] It was there, in his letters and in his personal influence, that he felt he could work best against what he feared: 'What I dread is *haste*—if full time is given for the Synodal Fathers to learn and reflect on the state of the case, I have little doubt they will keep clear of the dangerous points.'[31] But it was precisely the lack of time which the militants were working for.[32]

27. *Ward* II, pp. 279, 282.
28. *Ibid.*, p. 240.
29. *Ibid.*, p. 283.
30. *Orat.*, vol. 44, letters 40 and 41.
31. *Ward* II, p. 283.
32. For an excellent account not only of the Council but also of the necessary background material to make the struggle understandable, see C. Butler, *The Vatican Council: 1869–1870*, London, 1962.

In the meantime, the militants were fortifying their position. Newman received a report from Odo Russell on a conversation he had had in Rome with Cardinal Antonelli. The cardinal rejected the statement that the Council would be asked to define as a 'new' dogma the pope's infallibility:

> The Pope need not ask the Council whether he is infallible since God has made him so . . . The Council is a Parlement very like yours in England, for the discussion and reform of disciplinary questions. But Articles of Faith cannot be questioned or discussed. They come from God to the Pope, who himself has no choice; he must make the will of God known to the church as he is His vicar . . . The Council has nothing to do with articles of faith or dogmatic questions—these the Pope settles and proclaims without the Council, according to his conscience, which in those matters has always been infallible.[33]

Dupanloup became alarmed at these signs and wrote a letter to his clergy, attacking both Manning and Ward.[34] He maintained that the pope was indeed infallible, but that 'the exact knowledge of what he taught infallibly, and when he taught infallibly, came to the faithful, in the cases which his own words might well leave doubtful, not through the rapid private judgment of an individual, however able, or of a single public writer for his readers, but through the gradual operation of the learning and knowledge of the Church as a whole'.[35] In this view of the matter, the bishop of Orleans agreed fully with Newman; the whole Church was needed in order to teach, whether infallibly or not.[36]

As the Council assembled and it became more and more clear that the definition was going to be attempted, Newman made his feelings known. 'He was . . . in the full sense of the term an "Inopportunist". He objected to the definition of the decree, primarily because he regarded it as in the circumstances inopportune.'[37] He felt strongly, as we have seen, that the *circumstances* of the decree must also be considered. In fact the decree did turn out to be a compromise, and in that sense it can be called

33. *Orat.*, vol. 44, letter 14.
34. *Ward* II, p. 286.
35. *Ibid.*, pp. 286–7.
36. *Ibid.*
37. F. L. Cross, *J. H. Newman*, p. 150; see also C. S. Dessain, 'Cardinal Newman and Ecumenism' in *The Clergy Review* 50 (1965) 196, and F. Willam, 'Kardinal Newman und das erste vatikanische Konzil' in *Orientierung* 26 (1962) 175.

minimalistic.[38] In a letter to Mrs Froude on 21 November 1869 he goes into this matter:

> I have always held the Pope's Infallibility as an opinion, and am not therefore likely to feel any personal anxiety as to the result of this Council. Still I am strongly opposed to its definition— and for this reason. Hitherto nothing has been ever done at Councils but what is *neeessary*; what is the necessity of this? There is no heresy to be put down. It is a dangerous thing to go beyond the rule of tradition in such a matter. In the early times the Nicean Council gave rise to dissentions and to confusion which lasted near a century. The Council of Ephesus opened a question which it took three centuries to settle. Well, these Councils were necessary—they were called to resist and condemn opposition to our Lord's divinity—heresies—they could not be helped. But why is the Pope's Infallibility to be defined? even, if denying it was a heresy, which no one says, how many do deny it? do they preach it? are they making converts to it? Let us look to it lest a judgment come down upon us, if we do, *though we have a right to do*, what we ought not to do. We must not play with edged tools. I am against the definition because it opens a long controversy. You cannot settle the question by a word—whatever is passed, must be a half, a quarter measure. Archbishop Manning himself only aims at *condemning two propositions*, i.e. a negation act. How will that *decide* the question? No—it only opens it. At Nicaea, and Ephesus, great questions were opened, only opened. They had, as I have said, been by heretics first. Now, the Bishops of the Church are called upon to take the first step in opening a question as difficult, and not as justifiable, as the question which those early Councils were to discuss. This question will lead to an alteration of the elementary constitution of the Church. Our one doctrine, in which all doctrines are concluded, is, 'The Church's word is to be believed—'. Hitherto 'the Church's decision' means that of the Pope and the Bishops—now it is proposed to alter this for 'the Pope's word'. It is an alteration of the fundamental dogma . . . If anything could throw religion into confusion, make sceptics, encourage scoffers, and throw back inquirers, it will be the definition of this doctrine. This I shall think even if it passes—

38. Cross, *J. H. Newman*, p. 153.

because, though the doctrine must be inwardly received as true, its definition may still be most unreasonable and unwise. I do not know that the Church is protected against inexpedient acts—though of course God overrules them.[39]

This is one of Newman's most complete and clear statements of his position. His point was expressed in the question: 'When has definition of a doctrine *de fide* been a luxury of devotion and not a stern painful necessity?'[40] Newman, according to Ward, often told his dear friend Lord Emly that his main objection, as the last letter showed, was not to '*a* definition on the subject, but to such a definition as was likely to be passed in the haste in which matters were proceeding and to exaggerations of its import which extremists were likely to propagate'.[41] For Newman, the 'Church moves as a whole; it is not a mere philosophy, it is a communion . . .'.[42] As a whole, the Church needs time to gather its mind, to assemble its resources; if this is not allowed, then one is playing with fire: 'and this is the great charge which I bring against the immediate authors of the movement, that *they have not given us time* . . . the beginning and end of my thoughts about this Council is "You are going too fast, You are going too fast".'[43]

Whether too fast or not, the definition was passed on 18 July 1870. Eighty-eight bishops who had cast *non placet* votes in the general congregation held before the formal promulgation, and sixty-two who had given *placet juxta modum* votes, sent a letter to the pope explaining their move. They then left Rome before the formal vote, so as to avoid an open clash with the pope.[44] Newman, when he heard of the results, was thunderstruck; he had not seen the text, and was not aware of the mild tone its opponents had been able to give it.[45] He was in some indecision as to whether it was

39. *Orat.,* vol. 44, letter 39.
40. *Ward* II, p. 288; this is from Newman's famous letter to his bishop at the Council; for its complete text, see Appendix, p. 140, below.
41. *Ibid.,* p. 295; this certainly is more than J. C. Fenton's thesis can bear ('Newman and Papal Infallibility' in *American Essays for the Newman Centenial,* p. 166). Fenton contends that 'Newman's polemic against Ward and Manning was directed primarily not against an exaggerated or an extremist notion of papal infallibility, but against its presentation or definition as Catholic dogma'. If Fenton had looked a bit more closely, he would have seen that the situation was exactly the opposite.
42. *Ward* II, p. 296.
43. *Orat.,* vol. 45, letter 31 to P. Coleridge, 13 April 1870.
44. *Ward* II, p. 303, where the text of the bishops' letter can be found.
45. *Ibid.,* pp. 307–8.

binding immediately or not, due to the fact that the Council had not yet come to an end. He wanted to wait and see what the bishops who constituted the rather large minority at the Council would do, for he felt that a council divided against itself would be very questionable in its acts.[46] But there was never a thought as to leaving the Church, or not accepting the decree:

> But no thing which has taken place justifies separation from the One Church . . . The Church is the Mother of high and low— of the ruler as well as the ruled. *Securus judicat orbis terrarum.* If she declares by her various voices that the Pope is infallible in certain matters, in those matters infallible he is. When Bishops and people say all over the earth that is the truth, whatever complaint we may rightly have against certain ecclesiastical proceedings, let us not oppose ourselves to the universal voice.[47]

Newman, even in this matter which seems to go against him, appeals to the whole Church and finds that if it witnesses to what he had opposed, then he must bend before its voice. In fact, the minority, for all practical purposes, did not take arms against the decision, but made their peace with the Church and accepted the Council's decree.

Confronted with the prospect of a schism, men such as Dupanloup and Hefele submitted and promulgated the Council's acts in their dioceses.[48] These steps removed what little scruples Newman may still have had as regards the definition. Added to that was the book by Bishop Fessler,[49] who, as the Secretary General of the Council, certainly carried an authoritative voice. His was a most moderate view, and together with the constitution *Pastor aeternus* and its historical introduction as written by Fränzelin and Kleutgen,[50] Newman had no compunction at accepting the decree. But the action of the majority at the Council left him scandalized, and their statements after the Council were scarcely in line with the definition as passed. He felt a great duty to put this situation right, as far as he could. Within four years, he was to take up his pen once more in defense of the whole Church as opposed to an exaggerated church within a church.

46. *Ibid.,* pp. 308–9.
47. *Orat.,* vol. 45, letter 4 to P. Hyacinthe, 22 November 1870.
48. *Ward* II, p. 372.
49. *Die wahre und falsche Unfehlbarkeit der Päpste,* Vienna, 1871.
50. *Ward* II, pp. 306–7.

14

The Gladstone Controversy

It is only fitting that we close this study of Newman's thought on the teaching function of the Church with a consideration, albeit brief, of his last controversial writing, his *Letter to the Duke of Norfolk*.[1] We will find him rounding the edges of his views and bringing them into the harmony he had searched for all his life.

Fessler's book on papal infallibility[2] countenanced the views Newman himself took of the proceedings at the Council, and he felt relieved that a man of such authority would render this service to the Church. Fessler especially pointed out the necessity of not forgetting the *schola theologorum* as the essential link in securing the 'constitution of the Church against absolutism and the excesses of individuals'.[3] Newman himself acquiesced in this view of the matter, saying that 'the truth being that the Schola Theologorum is (in the Divine Purpose, *I* should say) the regulating principle of of the Church . . .'.[4] He felt now, more than ever, that the pope's infallibility, if it meant anything, meant only that 'A Pope is not inspired; he has not an inherent gift of divine knowledge. When he speaks *ex cathedra,* he may say little or much, but he is simply protected from saying what is untrue.'[5]

In other words, the pope does not himself exercise the whole teaching function of the Church. He is protected from error in giving an authentic witness to the original revelation. But the limitations and qualifications necessary for this to come into play and yield an infallible declaration practically force him into interaction with the rest of the Church. Thus for Newman the

1. See F. S. Stangl, *J. H. Newman's Doctrine of Papal Infallibility in the Gladstone Controversy,* for a complete coverage of the question.
2. *Die wahre und falsche Unfehlbarkeit der Päpste,* Vienna, 1871.
3. *Ward* II, p. 373.
4. *Ibid.,* p. 374.
5. *Ibid.,* p. 378.

role of the *schola* is one of great weight; it determines the extent and exactness of papal pronouncements. 'No truth stands by itself—each is kept in order and harmonized by other truths.'[6]

After the Council, Newman returned to the project of republishing all his works in a uniform edition. The thought of writing again did not cross his mind, and he felt that, with his previous works put in final form, he could make ready for the end. Yet he still had a nagging feeling that there was something he might do to aid the Church in its coming time of trouble. He had never written, however, without a call to battle; without such a stimulus he felt that he simply could not write.[7] The call came very quickly. Gladstone wrote an attack on the Catholic community of England; Newman proved to be the only man in a position to answer it.[8]

Gladstone took the Vatican decrees to mean that the spirit of absolutist centralization was being driven to its furthest conclusions; that the thought and policies of men such as Ward, Manning and Veuillot were now in formal use by Catholics.[9] Newman immediately saw this as an opportunity to answer those thinkers under the cloak of an answer to Gladstone:

> Gladstone's excuse is, I suppose, the extravagance of Archbishop Manning in his 'Caesarism', and he will do us a service if he gives us an opportunity of speaking. We can speak against Gladstone, while it would not be decent to speak against Manning. The difficulty is *who* ought to speak?[10]

Earlier, in a letter to Lady Simeon, Newman had said that Manning 'is fearfully exaggerating what has been done at the Council'; he goes on to label this 'an enormous tyranny' on the part of his metropolitan.[11] But he hesitated to reply himself. It would be most difficult to do so without giving offence in high quarters.[12] At last he was won over to take on the task:

> I had for a long time been urged by my friends to write—but I

6. *Ibid.*, p. 379.

7. *Ibid.*, pp. 398–400.

8. Gladstone's original pamphlet was entitled *The Vatican Decrees in Their Bearing on Civil Allegiance. A Political Expostulation*, London, 1874.

9. *Ward* II, p. 402.

10. *Ibid.*

11. Dated 18 November 1870, in C. S. Dessain, 'What Newman taught in Manning's Church' (in *Infallibility in the Church and Anglican-Catholic Dialogue*, A. M. Farrer *et al.*, London, 1968), p. 61.

12. *Ward* II, p. 403.

persisted in saying that I would not go out of my way to do so. When Gladstone wrote, I saw it was now or never, and I had so vivid an apprehension that I should get into a great trouble and rouse a great controversy round me, that I was most unwilling to take up my pen . . .[13] I had made a compact with myself, that, if I did write, I would bring out my whole mind, and specially speak out on the subject of what I had in a private letter called an 'insolent and aggressive faction'—so that I wrote and printed, I may say, in much distress of mind.[14]

The pamphlet, addressed as a letter to the young Duke of Norfolk, appeared in January of 1875 and was an immediate success. One of many statements attesting to its success is from Father Harper sj to Mr Todd:

> I look upon it as Newman's *chef-d'oeuvre*. It is gigantically grand, built up on a sound, accurate, deep theology . . . he seems to have written it with one eye raised to God, the other fixed on his pen.[15]

A week later Newman was told that:

> Your letter to the Duke of Norfolk is the only thing we can talk about . . . All the Catholics with whom I have spoken regarded your letter to the Duke as our future textbook.[16]

And Bishop Ullathorne, Newman's ordinary, wrote to Rome:

> *Quod maxime importat in hoc opusculo est alta et vigorosa confessio scriptoris de ejus fide in respectu infallibilitatis Pontificis.*[17]

Ward summarized Newman's argument in these words:

> Newman did not insist primarily on denying to this or that Pontifical document the character of an *ex cathedra* utterance, but rather argued that the determination as to precisely what was defined irreformably in such utterances appertained solely to the Schola Theologorum and was a matter of time. The issue he chiefly dwelt on was not the authority of this or that Pontifical document, but the precise scope of what it determined.[18]

13. *Ibid.*, pp. 407–8.
14. *Ibid.*
15. *Orat.*, vol. 49; dated 7 January 1875.
16. *Ibid.*, dated 16 January 1875.
17. *Ibid.*, letter 50.
18. *Ward* II, p. 406.

It is to this thought of Newman's on the role played by the whole
Church in its deliberations, even in the infallible deliberations of
a pope or council, that we now turn.

The views being propagated at that time in England 'might be
dismissed as being of merely historical interest but for the fact that
they became so prevalent in the Catholic Church for the next
ninety years'. Therefore 'surely we must welcome any authoritative
teacher who puts them in perspective . . .'[19] Seen in this light, the
whole controversy becomes meaningful to our time, and Newman's
thought takes on more weight; for, in respect to infallibility,
Newman's 'view of the subject . . . like so much else of his teaching,
has been vindicated at the Second Vatican Council'.[20]

Newman begins immediately, stating that 'None but the *Schola
Theologorum* is competent to determine the force of Papal and
Synodal utterances, and the exact interpretation of them is a work
of time.'[21] For Newman there is no isolated element in the Church
which works by itself. The pope may possess his gift of infallibility
in se; but in possessing it *as* the pope, he is also bound to the
Church, both in its past and in its present: he is always pope *of* the
Church, not simply pope. In accenting the role of the *schola,*
Newman wants to make this point clear. In a letter of 28 July 1875,
he goes into the matter in detail:

> . . . there are no words, ever so clear, but require an interpretation,
> at least as to their extent. For instance, an inspired writer says
> that 'God is love'—but supposing a set of men so extend this
> as to conclude—'*therefore* there is no future punishment for bad
> men?' Some power then is needed to determine the general
> sense of authoritative words—to determine their direction,
> drift, limits, and comprehension, to hinder gross perversions.
> This power is virtually the *passive infallibility* of the whole body
> of the Catholic people. The active infallibility lies in the Pope
> and Bishops—the passive in the 'universitas' of the faithful.
> Hence the maxim 'securus judicat orbis terrarum'. The body

19. See Dessain, 'What Newman taught in Manning's Church', p. 60.
20. *Ibid.*, p. 62; cf. *Lumen Gentium*, n. 12: *Populus Dei sanctus de munere quoque
prophetico Christi participat . . . vivum Eius testimonium maxime per vitam
fidei ac caritatis . . . Universitas fidelium, qui unctionem habent a Sancto, in credendo
falli nequit atque hanc suam peculiarem proprietatem mediante supernaturali sensu fidei
totius populi manifestat, cum 'ab Episcopis usque ad extremos laicos fideles' universalem
suum consensum de rebus fidei et morum exhibet.*
21. *Ang. Diff.* II, p. 170.

of the faithful never can misunderstand what the Church determines by the gift of its active infallibility. Here on the one hand I observe that a local sense of a doctrine, held in this or that country, is not a 'sensus universitatis', and on the other hand the Schola Theologorum is one chief portion of that universitas—and it acts with great force both in correcting popular misapprehensions and narrow views of the teaching of the active *infallibilitas,* and, by the intellectual investigations and disputes which are its very life, it keeps the distinction clear between theological opinion, and is the antagonist of dogmatism. And while the differences of the School maintain the liberty of thought, the unanimity of its members is the safeguard of the infallible decisions of the Church and the champion of faith.[22]

This is a beautifully clear statement of Newman's meaning as he brought it out in his *Letter to the Duke of Norfolk.* Both aspects of the Church's teaching activity—the hierarchy as the active infallible element and the body of the faithful in its passive infallible role—bear witness to each other, the difference being that the active infallible aspect determines the extent and meaning of the witness borne by the passive infallible element; and yet the latter must then work in determining the determination put forth by the active infallible element of the Church, as measured against the original witness.

Newman at first works out his thought on the papacy. For him it is a historical fact that cannot be played with: 'We must take things as they are; to believe in a Church, is to believe in the Pope ... That which in substance was possessed by the Nicene Hierarchy, that the Pope claims now.'[23]

This shift from the possessions of the Church to the possessions of the pope is in the name of unity; the Church would lose its note of unity without the unifying presence of the pope. 'We should not believe in the Church at all, unless we believe in its visible head.'[24] Without that visible center of unity, the Church itself would lose its character as a community, *one* community, entrusted with the revelation of God. Thus it is not so much the pope as possessor of these claims, but the Church itself which is attacked in Gladstone's words, as Newman carefully points out:

22. *Ward* II, p. 564.
23. *Ang. Diff.* II, p. 208.
24. *Ibid.*

That concentration of the Church's powers which history brings before us ought not to be the simple object of his indignation. It is not the existence of a Pope, but of a Church, which is his aversion. It is the powers themselves, and not their distribution and allocation in the ecclesiastical body which he writes against.[25]

This brings Newman to a discussion of the powers themselves. He contends that his argument does not demand the conclusion that the popes are always right; on the contrary, history teaches us that popes have been wrong, that at times they were resisted—and rightly so.[26] The pope's sovereignty, according to Newman, is not limitless; his task is to give an 'explanation, and, in a certain sense, limitation, of what I have hitherto been saying concerning the Church's and the Pope's powers'.[27]

Now this authority of the pope, and of the bishops, is to be obeyed; Newman does not waver in his loyalty to church authority.[28] But this obedience owed to papal authority does not rob the individual of his own moral responsibility. Newman does 'not see what the Pope takes away at all from our private consciences'.[29] The obedience demanded of the faithful to the pope's authority is required in order to preserve the unity of that body entrusted with revelation as a message to bear to the world.[30] Thus there is no such thing as absolute obedience, which must be given to either a civil power, or to the pope; for 'if either the Pope or the Queen demanded of me an "Absolute Obedience", he or she would be transgressing the laws of human society. I give an absolute obedience to neither'.[31] Such a demand would run counter to the presence of God's law implanted within us in the form of conscience.[32]

'Conscience', reiterates Newman, 'is the aboriginal Vicar of Christ.'[33] As such, it is the basis for both the position of the pope in his authority, as well as for the ultimate responsibility of the individual; for,

25. *Ibid.*, pp. 209–10.
26. *Ibid.*, pp. 216–17.
27. *Ibid.*, p. 223.
28. *Ibid.*, pp. 225–6.
29. *Ibid.*, p. 231.
30. *Ibid.*, p. 236.
31. *Ibid.*, p. 243.
32. *Ibid.*, pp. 246–7.
33. *Ibid.*, p. 248.

Did the Pope speak against Conscience in the true sense of the word, he would commit a suicidal act. He would be cutting the ground from under his feet. His very mission is to proclaim the moral law . . . On the law of conscience and its sacredness are founded both his authority in theory and his power in fact.[34]

Thus Gladstone's main contention—that the pope's infallibility makes moral slaves out of all Catholics—falls to the ground. Newman has pointed out one of the limitations put upon the teaching authority of the Church: the divine law of God as expressed in the individual's conscience. Only in this light are his words to be interpreted:

Certainly, if I am obliged to bring religion into after-dinner toasts, (which indeed does not seem quite the thing) I shall drink—to the Pope, if you please,—still, to Conscience first, and to the Pope afterwards.[35]

Turning to those statements termed infallible, Newman ascertains that this note of infallibility is a divine *assistentia,* simply ensuring against untruth. But the pope's 'acts and his words on doctrinal subjects must be carefully scrutinized and weighed, before we can be sure what really he has said'.[36] It has been said that this is Newman's weakest section in his writings, that his interpretation of the decrees of Vatican I is 'an imperfect and inexact statement of the conciliar doctrine'.[37] In this view, Newman's problem was that 'the only matter of moment . . . is the fact that the Church itself is infallible'.[38] This is a completely falsified view of Newman's position. In accepting the Vatican decrees, he indeed invoked the whole Church:

If the definition is consistently received by the whole body of the faithful, as valid, or as the expression of a truth, then too it will claim our assent by the force of the great dictum, 'Securus judicat orbis terrarum'. This indeed is a broad principle by which all acts of the rulers of the Church are ratified.[39]

34. *Ibid.,* p. 252.
35. *Ibid.,* p. 261.
36. *Ibid.,* p. 280.
37. J. Fenton, 'Newman and Papal Infallibility', p. 163.
38. *Ibid.,* p. 167.
39. *Ang. Diff.* II, p. 303.

To avoid misunderstandings, Newman added an explanation of the word 'ratify' in the second edition; by this he meant 'brought home to us as authentic'.[40] That is, if it is borne witness to by the whole Church, in its role as bearer of the message of revelation; if it is stamped by those who bear witness to the truth, not just the hierarchy but the body of the faithful, as authentically determined by the infallible statement of the pope or the Church.

İt is not an agreement, but a matter of fact which is here at stake: the determining statement of the pope, delineating the witness of the whole Church, is in turn borne witness to. This witness will continue, though popes will pass: 'There is nothing of course that can be reversed in the definitions of the Vatican Council; but the series of its acts was cut short by the great war, and, should the need arise (which is not likely) to set right a false interpretation, another Leo will be given us for the occasion.'[41] It will remain till the end of time, that 'legacy of truth, of which the Church, in all her members, but especially in her hierarchy, is the divinely appointed trustee'.[42]

Newman completes his discussion with a look at just how the Church operates in the presence of an infallible statement from the chair of Peter. Hardly has the Church 'spoken out magisterially some great general principle, when she sets her theologians to work to explain her meaning in the concrete, by strict interpretation of its wording, by the illustration of its circumstances, and by the recognition of exceptions, in order to make it as tolerable as possible, and the least of a temptation, to self-willed, independent, or wrongly educated minds'.[43]

We see here 'what caution is to be observed, on the part of private and unauthorized persons, in imposing upon the consciences of others any interpretation of dogmatic enunciations which is beyond the legitimate sense of the words, inconsistent with the principle that all general rules have exceptions, and unrecognized by the Theological *Schola*'.[44] And this is precisely what a misunderstanding of Newman would do; reflecting the same mind as Manning, it would brand all not in agreement with it as either incompetent or disloyal to the Catholic faith. Such a

40. *Ibid.*, p. 372.
41. *Ibid.*, p. 307.
42. *Ibid.*, p. 314.
43. *Ibid.*, p. 321.
44. *Ibid.*, pp. 337–8.

view attributes to Newman the 'bizarre thesis that the final determination of what is really condemned in an authentic ecclesiastical pronouncement is the work of private theologians, rather than of the particular organ of the *ecclesia docens,* which has actually formulated the condemnation . . . This tendency to consider the pronouncements of the *ecclesia docens,* and particularly the statements of papal encyclicals, as utterances which must be interpreted for the Christian people, rather than explained to them, is definitely harmful to the Church.'[45]

But is it not rather, as we have seen in the example of Newman, that 'the Pope defines on principle only what is already believed, as revealed in the Church. And, in fact the actual faith of the Church as a whole was ascertained before the doctrines of the Immaculate Conception and later the Assumption were defined.'[46] Is it not true that this process of belief, bearing witness to the revelation entrusted to the whole Church, goes on, bearing witness to the utterances of the authoritative Church, against which even the infallible statements of a pope must be measured? Is it not true that a position which treats the witnessing Church as mindless children who are to have all explained to them from on high, instead of recognizing their place in the one Church of Jesus Christ, tends toward the one thing Newman feared in the definition of papal infallibility, i.e. the building of a church within a church? Is it not true that the unity of the Church, which every one of us is bound to preserve and strengthen, is best served in a teaching Church which functions as a *whole,* witnessing to the one faith given it from Christ, until the end of time?

Newman certainly thought so; he worked the whole of his long and fruitful life for harmony and balance in the Church's teaching action. For him the Church was the 'pillar and the ground of truth'; but only as the one Church was it so, and to this task everyone is called who comes to this Church and finds there that faith which saves. Here it is that Newman closed the circle of his many-faceted thought: the unity of authority, the freedom of diversity were to live in organic harmony, witnessing the revelation of God in Christ to the world.[47]

45. Fenton, 'The Doctrinal Authority of Papal Encyclicals', p. 220.
46. Dessain, 'What Newman taught in Manning's Church', p. 76.
47. J. Guitton, *Mitbürgern der Wahrheit,* p. 140.

Newman and the Magisterium Today

If we are to evaluate properly the contribution of Newman's thought to the present turmoil and study surrounding the Church's teaching function, we must first take into account the historical development—both speculatively and practically—of this aspect of the Church's activity since Newman's time. The recent issuance of the papal encyclical *Humanae Vitae,* and its varied reception around the world, make it imperative that we first view the developments of the past hundred years, before attempting to analyse the present situation. What we are experiencing now is not an isolated phenomenon, totally dependent upon vagaries of this particular moment, but belongs to a much larger pattern which has been unfolding with increasing rapidity over the last century. In this last chapter, therefore, we will first sketch briefly the historical development of the magisterium from the First Vatican Council to our present position; then we will analyse that position in the light of Newman's thought as brought out in the preceding chapters.[1]

As Newman had predicted, the effects of the Vatican I definition of papal infallibility were anything but calming. Newman's controversy with Gladstone in England was but one of many which raged throughout the Catholic world.[2] As he had predicted, a great storm broke out over the definition; several of the leading bishops who had been in the minority in Rome hesitated for long periods of time before proclaiming the acts of the Council in their

1. For more detailed information on the various stages of the magisterium's development over the past hundred years, see the pertinent articles in the *Lexikon für Theologie und Kirche* and in the *New Catholic Encyclopedia,* and the expanded bibliographies given there.
2. See chapter 14, above.

dioceses, and Döllinger was excommunicated in 1871.[3] Only months after the ending of the Council a movement towards organized opposition was under way; it culminated in the founding of the Old Catholics.[4] All these events had a common source: a fear that papal infallibility, now under the sanction of an ecumenical council, would lead to a dangerous and one-sided exaggeration of the Church's teaching function in respect to its power of definition. As we saw during our discussion of Newman's involvement with Vatican I, the efforts of such men as Ward and Veuillot were certainly not helping to allay such fears. What had actually happened?

At the beginning of the nineteenth century, a Protestant canon lawyer, Georg Phillips, introduced Catholic theology to the theory of three ecclesiastical powers to match the three offices of the Church given it by Christ.[5] This was new material for Roman theologians; up to that time they had used only the two-power theory of Aquinas, ignoring the Protestant tradition—stemming from Calvin—of the three offices of Christ.[6] In the short span of time before the First Vatican Council, the Catholic theological world was able to digest this theory to such a degree that the Council's official acts and documents show clearly an acceptance of three offices of the Church together with the power particular to each office.[7] Nevertheless traces of Aquinas's theory of two powers were to be found again and again in the Council's work, but always under the stress of trying to fit in the functions of the three offices of sanctification, governance and teaching; the magisterium ended up being understood as *pars et species* of the Church's jurisdictional power.[8]

It is against this background that the definition of papal

3. See Newman's letter to Ullathorne during the Council, Appendix, p. 140; see also Butler, *The Vatican Council*, pp. 417–48; on Döllinger's excommunication see I. von Döllinger, *Briefe und Erklärungen über die vatikanischen Dekrete 1869 bis 1887*, Darmstadt, 1968, pp. 100–102.

4. See Butler, *op. cit.*, p. 427.

5. See G. Phillips, *Kirchenrecht*, vol. 2, Regensburg, 1846, p. 137; also the introductory chapter of J. Fuchs, *Vom Wesen der kirchlichen Lehrgewalt*, diss. masch., Münster, 1946.

6. See E. F. K. Müller's article, 'Jesu Christi dreifaches Amt' in Hauck, *Realenzyklopädie für protestantische Theologie und Kirche*, vol. 8[3], pp. 733–41; also K. Mörsdorf, 'Ecclesiastical Authority' in *Sacramentum Mundi*, vol. 1, New York, 1968, pp. 133–9.

7. See J. Fuchs, *op. cit.*, p. 96.

8. *Ibid.*, pp. 97, 100.

infallibility passed the Council. It is also against this background
that we must see the pastoral letters of the German and Swiss
episcopates; these were strong attempts to reassert a balance into
the Church's teaching office by emphatically delineating the
necessary role of the bishops *and* the whole Church in its teaching
activity.[9] As Newman had forecast, efforts were under way to
'trim the boot'; the pope was not to be allowed to act isolated and
alone, appropriating the Church's teaching authority to himself:
safeguards, reestablishing a healthy balance *within*, not without,
the Church, were needed.[10] Nor could the relegation of the
Church's teaching function to an aspect of its jurisdictional power
hope to aid this effort. In doing so, the Church's teaching office
was being reduced to a matter of law and obedience; such an understanding completely dismissed the element of the freedom of
Christian witness in faith, an essential note for which Paul had
fought so hard, and which Newman had attempted to reintroduce
into the main stream of nineteenth-century theology. And it was
this concern which provided one of Modernism's leading motifs.

As we now know, Modernism never existed in the form of a
unified school of thought, or as a systematized movement on the
international scene.[11] Instead, it consisted of a few men's efforts
to confront what they felt were the most essential questions posed
to the Church by the modern age ushered in with the end of the
nineteenth century; and they proposed to do this within, not
without the confines of the Church.[12] One of their deepest concerns was expressed in a desire that theology and the life of the
Church should return to its primary sources. In France, Alfred
Loisy attempted to revitalize an almost moribund Catholic
exegesis in an effort to recover, as purely as possible, the original
and most basic meaning of Jesus's message.[13] Such work would
inevitably lead to speculation on the Church's teaching function;
but it was in England, with the appearance of George Tyrrell, that
the magisterium was rigorously subjected to a review.[14]

9. For the text of the German pastoral and excerpts of the Swiss letter, see
Butler, *op. cit.,* pp. 427–31 and 464 respectively.
10. See Appendix, p. 142, below.
11. For a thorough bibliography, see J. Ratté, *Three Modernists,* New York,
1967, pp. 353–61.
12. *Ibid.,* pp. 13–15; also R. Adolphs, *The Church is Different,* London, 1966,
p. 26.
13. Adolphs, *op. cit.,* p. 23.
14. For our purposes his last work, *Christianity at the Crossroads,* posthumously
published in 1909 and reprinted in 1963, will serve best.

Tyrrell rejected the so-called 'new orthodoxy', which in regard to the Church's teaching function consisted of ecumenical councils turned into theological debates.[15] In his eye, this new view saw the magisterium as 'deducing the logical consequences of the faith of past generations, and adding them to the evergrowing body of explicit and actual beliefs'.[16]

The so-called 'old orthodoxy', however, was based on the 'infallible memory of the faithful collectively'; in order to know the faith, you did not argue about it, you observed it: what did the people in fact believe; what was the people's faith as witnessed to by the bishops together.[17] There was no real development possible in the area of true doctrine; the Church's collective memory simply recalled what had been committed to its care by Jesus. Doctrinal definitions on the part of the Church did not decide that a matter was *de fide*; they simply declared that a matter had *always* been *de fide*.[18]

But Tyrrell also rejected the 'old orthodoxy'; it had crumbled to dust under the pressure of history and the advance of knowledge, and was incapable of supporting modern man in his faith.[19] Yet in formulating his theory of the Church's retention and passing on of Jesus's message, Tyrrell took great pains in preserving the two essential elements of the 'old orthodoxy': the *whole* Church *witnessing* to its faith. The basis for any religion is the individual's religious experience; for Christianity it is precisely the universality of the faith experience in Jesus which allows it to teach this faith. Although—and this was the heart of Tyrrell's new theory—this experience may radically change from generation to generation, from epoch to epoch, still it remains the foundation for Christianity's teaching function. The collective memory of the faithful, remembering under the correction of its here-and-now, present experience of its given faith in Jesus, is the only organ able to present the message of that faith.[20] No hierarchy may separate itself from this collective memory of the faithful and pretend to declare what is faith, and what is not. Only as the servant—the mouthpiece—of the whole body of the faithful witnessing to the faith may the hierarchical structures of the Church assume a role in the activities of any magisterial effort.

15. G. Tyrrell, *Christianity at the Crossroads,* p. 37.
16. *Ibid.*
17. *Ibid.;* see also Vatican II, *Lumen Gentium,* n. 12.
18. Tyrrell, *op. cit.,* p. 33.
19. *Ibid.,* p. 40.
20. *Ibid.,* p. 144.

Rome's reaction was swift and hard; Tyrrell was excommunicated and his books placed on the Index; his theory was explicitly condemned in Pius x's decrees against Modernism.[21] There was to be no encroachment upon the power of the hierarchically constituted magisterium to rule supreme in controlling the Church's teaching function. Vatican I had legally established a gross imbalance in the Church's magisterial activities, and all attempts to right it and return it to its proper fullness were repulsed. It was not until World War II had convulsed mankind as no other catastrophe in history that once again the forces of balance began to stir within the Church.

With his encyclical *Aeterni Patris* in 1879 Leo XIII hoped for a return to the scholastic excellence displayed in Thomas Aquinas.[22] And indeed the first third of the twentieth century saw a renaissance in Thomistic studies. But coinciding with the advent of World War II, a movement came into its own which promised a fresh blossoming of variegated theological directions. New perspectives were taken up; problems laid forever to rest were resurrected to confront new knowledge; it was recognized that only one manner of viewing a matter could not do justice to its reality.[23] One of the prime concerns of this development was the place of divergent theological perspectives within the Church. Theologians became conscious once again of their active role both in the Church and in the world. One of Newman's fondest dreams was being realized: the *schola theologorum*, which he felt to be so important in the life of the Church, was once more throbbing with life.[24] Out of this so-called 'new theology' in the France and Germany of the 1940s arose essential questions regarding the nature of the theological enterprise and its place in the Church; it was only a matter of time before the Church's teaching function came under the eye of inspection.

Just as during the so-called Modernist crisis of the century's first decade, so also now the main impetus was supplied by a re-examination of the very concept of revelation itself.[25] In fact, it is

21. The decree *Lamentabili*, 3 July 1907 (Denzinger[31], n. 4, 22, 54, 58, 59); see also the encyclical *Pascendi dominici Gregis*, 8 September 1907 (Denzinger, n. 2079, 2091).
22. In AAS 11 (1878/79) 98ff, n. 31.
23. For a brief but excellent discussion of this development in France, see Y. M. Congar, *A History of Theology*, New York, 1968, pp. 7–20.
24. *Ibid.*, pp. 13–14.
25. *Ibid.*, pp. 12–13.

the difficulties and questions raised by such a re-examination which continue to form the nucleus of our decade's theological ferment. Such a preoccupation with revelation is bound to take up, sooner or later, the role of a teaching Church; if one is questioning the value of dogmatic formulas in themselves, then perforce the organ which forges and proclaims them becomes of great concern also.[26] As indicated, one of the fruits of this discussion was the reaffirmation of the essential and vital role played by the *schola theologorum*, an activity constituted by the myriad avenues of approach to points of theological reflection.

With Pius XII's encyclical *Humani Generis* in 1950, however, such speculation was, for the moment at least, effectively choked off.[27] Theologians were recalled to one standard of truth for the validity of their speculations: the magisterium.[28] For all practical purposes this standard was effectively equated with the voice of Rome.[29] Thus it was not the interaction of theologians all over the world, purifying their thought through dialogue with one another and with the faithful of the whole Church, which produced valid presentations of the Christian faith; rather it was the word of Rome alone which was capable of doing so.[30] As if to prove his point, two and one half months later Pius XII defined 'as a divinely revealed dogma' the assumption of Mary, body and soul, into heaven.[31] In the process, he ignored pleas from various corners of the theological world to reconsider his action, just as eighty years before Newman had pleaded with the fathers of Vatican I that they were 'going too fast'.[32] But Rome listened as little in 1950 as it had in 1870; even though no heresy was to be condemned the definition took place, appearing to have been more an 'expression of great solemnity and impressive glorification' than a necessity for the Church's life. This second occasion of the exercise of the pope's extraordinary magisterium presents a 'development which, if we are not mistaken, has been recognized as questionable and which most certainly will not become a general practice or habit'.[33]

26. *Ibid.*, pp. 9–10.
27. The text is to be found in AAS 42 (1950) 561–77.
28. See Denzinger[31], n. 2313.
29. *Ibid.*
30. *Ibid.*, n. 2313, 2314.
31. *Ibid.*, n. 2333.
32. *Orat.*, vol. 45, letter n. 31, to P. Coleridge, 13 April 1870.
33. O. Semmelroth, 'Zur Frage nach der Verbindlichkeit der dogmatischen Aussagen des Vatikanums II' in *Theologie und Philosophie* 42 (1967) 237.

The tide had turned since Vatican I, and the stream was now beginning to run towards Vatican II.

The calling of a council by John XXIII set loose a torrent of theological speculation; much was written and discussed as to the role of a council in the Church's life, and as to the function and place of the bishops and theologians who would work so intimately with its machinery. With these discussions as a background it was only natural that the Second Vatican Council would, at one point or another, concern itself with the teaching function of the Church. And indeed, scattered throughout the conciliar documents, many statements on the Church's magisterial activity are to be found. Yet as in all truly community efforts, compromise played a prominent role. The Dogmatic Constitution on the Church, for example, deals clearly with the prophetic function of all the faithful in the Christian community precisely in their witness to the faith; this witness of all the faithful—but only all the faithful together—cannot err.[34] One chapter later, however, papal infallibility in proclamation of doctrine is emphasized to such a degree that the very words of Vatican I are paraphrased.[35] Tacked onto this is a discussion of the role of the episcopal college in the Church's teaching effort. Throughout all of this no attempt is made to avoid the impression that these various elements have been quite inorganically strung together. The important thing, however, is that they were considered vital enough to the Church's teaching task to reach the level of conciliar formulation. And there is an even more important implication in their use.

According to John XXIII the Second Vatican Council was to have primarily a pastoral concern. This was not only to be manifested in its handling of discipline, but also and precisely in its magisterial activity.[36] This meant that, for all practical purposes, the procedure of dogmatic definition was to be avoided. This decision to express its thought and content in a manner devoid of formal doctrinal definitions allowed the Council to adopt a more flexible understanding of the Church's magisterium. Inherent in a formal declaration of dogma is a trans-historical understanding of the Church's teaching; but in the Council's eyes it is the historical and pilgrimage character of even the Church's teaching as regards

34. *Lumen Gentium*, n. 12; W. M. Abbott ed., *Documents of Vatican II*, p. 29.
35. *Ibid.*, n. 25; Abbott, *op. cit.*, pp. 48–9.
36. Abbott, *op. cit.*, p. 715.

faith and revelation which should be stressed. The Church teaches dynamically; it does not 'possess' the truth of faith in only one way, nor completely. In certain points, of course, the Council did intend to teach bindingly, but it did so dynamically, and not as if the last possible word had been spoken.[37] It is this recognition of the many-sided nature of the Church's teaching function that makes Vatican II so important in understanding the role of the magisterium in any future Church. The developments since the close of the Council must be seen in this light; they are attempts to make that recognition a living element in the Church's life, attempts to restore the balance and fullness of the teaching mission so essential to the Church's existence.

Two events since the end of the Council in 1965 have served to focus attention on the problematic of the Church's teaching function, and both are intimately related. The first was the announcement by Charles Davis, one of the foremost theologians of the English-speaking world and a *peritus* at the Council, that he was dissociating himself completely from the active ministry and the Roman Catholic Church; the second was the release, in July of 1968, of Paul VI's encyclical *Humanae Vitae* condemning all forms of artificial birth control. Both of these incidents have shaped the form of discussion centering on the Church's teaching function and, despite the shrill cries to be heard from all sides, have had a clarifying effect on the problems involved.

One of Davis's main reasons for leaving the Roman community was his contention that it was 'pervaded by a disregard for truth'.[38] Because of the nature of the Christian faith, Davis felt it essential that a church professing that faith have an unequivocal commitment to truth.[39] He interpreted his experience within the Roman church as proof that such a commitment to truth was, in fact, not present within this church, and that its pronouncements and teaching were primarily directed towards preserving an authoritative unity.[40] Davis saw this analysis exemplified to the fullest in the handling of the birth control issue. For him this was the epitome of the church's desire to relegate the search for truth to a secondary position in order to protect the doctrinal unity

37. Semmelroth, *op. cit.*, pp. 244–5.
38. C. Davis, *A Question of Conscience*, p. 64.
39. *Ibid.*, p. 65.
40. *Ibid.*, pp. 65, 69.

which guarantees the preservation of authority.[41] But Davis had written before the Pope's decision had been reached; with the issuance of *Humanae Vitae,* embodying Paul VI's long-awaited statement on the matter, the situation surrounding the exercise of the Church's teaching office became even more acute.

The Pope's publication of a solemn profession of faith a month before his decision on the birth control issue became known was to prepare the way for the acceptance of his final judgment.[42] It is indicative that he chose the form of a creed for this action. It was his hope that his birth control decision would be accepted within the context of doctrinal unity as expressed in his profession of faith. This, however, was not the case. An unprecedented storm of protest and dissent rose in opposition to the Pope's decision.[43] Not only did theologians raise their voices in not accepting the encyclical as a valid expression of the Church's teaching function, but many of the laity also refused to believe that contraception as practiced by them was morally wrong. What had been a moral question—the licitness of birth control—quickly degenerated into a vociferous dispute over the role and extent of a teaching office within the Church. In *Humanae Vitae* Pope Paul based his decision partly upon the contention that unity in belief is essential for the Christian Church, and that this unity can be achieved if all 'attend to the teaching office of the Church, and all speak the same language'.[44] In fact, this is simply begging the argument, for the possibility of a unity of doctrine as presented by a teaching office is the very point under dispute. The concluding remarks of this chapter, therefore, shall concern themselves with an investigation into several of Newman's insights concerning the teaching function of the Church, in the hope that they will prove beneficial in attempting to resolve the present situation surrounding the Church's teaching office.[45]

As we have seen, the practical understanding of the Church's teaching function is to provide for a unity of doctrinal belief. On the basis of one proclaimed teaching there will be only one

---

41. *Ibid.,* p. 93.
42. For the profession of faith, see AAS 60 (1968) 433–45.
43. 'Catholic Freedom vs Authority' in *Time,* 22 November 1968, p. 42.
44. *Humanae Vitae,* AAS 60 (1968) 481–503; 501, par. 28.
45. For a thorough discussion of the principle of disunity in Christian doctrine, see John Charlot, *New Testament Disunity,* New York: E. P. Dutton, 1970; this problematic forms the background to the rest of this chapter.

expressed faith. In fact, however, the idea of orthodoxy—*only one right* faith—emerged late in the history of theology, beginning to take form only in the third and fourth centuries.[46] Initially there were only 'heresies'—widely divergent Christian theologies, differing not only in the content of their interpretations, but also in the content of their initial givens.[47] But gradually the idea of an *orthodox* doctrine, especially as imposed by Rome, took hold; the teaching office became an instrument for preserving the politically oriented unity which Christianity's assumption of the governmental structures of the Roman empire had established. This development in the understanding of the Church's teaching function did not continue unabated through the centuries; various chapters in the history of theology poignantly illustrate the attempt to recover the teaching office from its wayward course. With Vatican I, however, and the definition of papal infallibility, Rome finally crowned its striving towards hegemony in doctrine with a seemingly unshakable capstone.[48] But history teaches us, as we saw above, that such a function may indeed *not* be the primary one of a teaching office in the Church. If in fact a unity of doctrine is an impossible goal—and recent studies of the New Testament would seem to indicate that such is the case[49]—the question that then begins to haunt our thoughts is, what purpose does a teaching function within a Christian community serve? The study of Newman's thought offered in this volume has introduced us to some important insights concerning this problem. Three of these key ideas may help us to come to grips with the present very problematical position of the Church's teaching office.[50] They are: the concept of *witness*; the concept of the *schola theologorum*; the concept of the *whole* Church.

The Church's role as witness to the faith was a major factor in Newman's early development.[51] It was his almost consuming

46. See W. Bauer, *Rechtgläubigkeit und Ketzerei im ältesten Christentum,* Tübingen, 1964[2], for a complete treatment of this point.
47. See Charlot, *op. cit.*
48. J. Neumann, 'Die Rechtsprinzipien des zweiten vatikanischen Konzils als Kritik an der traditionellen Kanonistik' in *Tübinger Quartalschrift* 147 (1967) 257–8.
49. See Charlot, *op. cit.*
50. A thorough presentation of the historical development of the Church's teaching office and a reassessment of its function in light of recent developments is being prepared by the author.
51. See above, chapters 2, 3, 4.

passion for the Fathers of the early Church which introduced him to the Christian community as constituted in giving witness to its faith in Christ. Particularly the Arian controversy of the fourth century impressed upon him the fact that the essentials of that faith in Christ were to be found in the witness of the community as a whole to its beliefs. The slim volume on primitive Christianity was entirely a testimonial of Newman's to this aspect of the Church's life. To his mind the faith in Christ was not primarily proclaimed and made alive by the theological pronouncements of authority, but rather in the very throb of the whole community's action on the basis of that faith. Authoritative utterances were not meant to teach those who did not yet know, but rather to reflect what already was both known and lived by the whole Church. Thus his anger at the proceedings of Vatican I: 'What have we done to be treated as the Faithful never were treated before?'[52] For him Catholics had not come to believe an article of their faith because it had been defined for them; rather 'it was defined because they believed it'.[53]

It is precisely this aspect of the Church's teaching function which has been neglected during the past hundred years. It is the whole Church's witness to *its* faith which is essentially constitutive of its teaching function, and not the witness of a small group within the community. Is it not possible that many misunderstandings which today cloud the actions of the Church's teaching office would be clarified if that teaching office were to take its proper place as the organ of expression to the whole community's witness to its faith? It is precisely the imbalance which has been introduced into the Church's teaching function which has caused so much irritation and dissent; the substitution of one aspect of the whole for that whole itself has been rejected by the Church. If the Church is to retain any teaching function at all it must return to the balanced view maintained by Newman in dependence upon the Church's oldest traditions: 'the two, the Church teaching and the Church taught, are put together, as one twofold testimony, illustrating each other, and never to be divided.'[54] This balance must again be regained with the magisterium, shorn of the unattractive trappings attached to that name, once more in a subordinate position, truly serving the whole Church, and faithfully

52. Newman to Ullathorne, Appendix, p. 140, below.
53. *Apol.*, p. 255.
54. *Consult. Faith.*, p. 71.

expressing the whole community's faith in its risen lord as given in its daily witness.

Newman attached great importance to the role played by the *scholà theologorum* in the development of the Church's teaching. He always thought it a disaster for theology that the great schools had been destroyed during the revolutions which began the nineteenth century:

> This age of the Church is peculiar,—in former times, primitive or medieval, there was not the extreme centralization which now is in use. If a private theologian said anything free, another answered him. If the controversy grew, then it went to a Bishop, a theological faculty, or to some foreign University. The Holy See was but the Court of ultimate appeal. *Now*, if I, as a private priest, put anything into print, Propaganda answers me at once. How can I fight with such a chain on my arm? It is like the Persians driven to fight under the lash. There was true private judgment in the primitive and medieval schools,—there are no schools now, no private judgment (in the religious sense of the phrase), no freedom, that is, of opinion. That is, no exercise of the intellect. No, the system goes on by the tradition of the intellect of former times. This is a way of things which, in God's own time, will work its cure, of necessity . . .[55]

It was his contention that the Church's doctrine only came to the fruition necessary for a teaching pronouncement through the work of the theologians scattered throughout the world. This *schola* is the middle step between the witness of the whole Church and the teaching office's expression of that witness. It represents the first level of reflection leading to an expression of the Church's faith.

But the *schola* is also the organ whereby the magisterium's statements are interpreted and sifted, to see whether they are truly an expression of the whole Church's witness. 'None', says Newman, 'but the "schola theologorum" is competent to determine the force of Papal and Synodal utterances, and the exact interpretation of them is a work of time.'[56] It is only the whole Church through the work of the *schola theologorum* which may interpret and

---

55. Newman to Miss Bowles, 19 May 1863; in *Ward* I, p. 588; see also Appendix, p. 139, below.
56. *Ang. Diff.* II, p. 170.

pass judgment on formal expressions of its witness to the faith.[57]

We find this point of Newman's sadly neglected in the present century. Newman himself felt uneasy about personal theological activity,[58] and the witch-hunts of the Modernist controversy and the unofficial condemnations preceding and following Pius XII's *Humani Generis* in 1950 were certainly not conducive to the fostering of that spirit of free investigation and speculation so necessary for the *schola theologorum* to function in its proper place within the Church. Even after the refreshing openness of Vatican II, leading scholars of the theological world still felt it necessary to issue a warning against the attempt to rob theologians of their newly recovered freedom.[59] They wanted to make it clear that the teaching office of the pope and bishops 'cannot and must not supersede, hamper and impede the teaching task of the theologians as scholars'.[60] But the teaching function of the Church will not regain its proper place in the Church's life until the theological enterprise as exercised by countless theologians throughout the world is accorded its free and full role in shaping, interpreting and determining those expressions of the magisterium which claim to reflect the witness of the whole Church.

Intimately connected with the notes of witness and of the *schola theologorum* is Newman's idea of the whole Church. As was seen in discussing these points, neither can be understood without reference to its foundation in the *whole* Church; it is essential for Newman that the totality of the Church's reality be the determination of its actions and life. It is not simply the witness of the faithful; nor is it the activity of the *schola theologorum*; neither is it the formal teaching of the hierarchical teaching office; rather the Church's teaching function is a result of all of these aspects of the Church's life brought together in one action. Perhaps, as has been recently suggested, it would be better to speak of a plurality of teaching offices:

Neither the magisterium nor the Church is simply hierarchical. In fact, since there are and should be various agencies of witness

---

57. See H. Hammans, 'Recent Catholic Views on Development of Dogma' in *Concilium* 1 (1967) 60; also W. Kasper, 'The Relationship between Gospel and Dogma' in *Concilium* 1 (1967) 75.
58. See above, footnote 55.
59. 'Scholars Plead for Theological Freedom' in *National Catholic Reporter*, Kansas City, 1 January 1969, p. 3.
60. *Ibid.*

and influence in the Church, it would be better to speak of the magisteria of the Church. We would then consider not just the papal and episcopal magisteria but the equally authentic magisterium of the laity and the magisterium of the theologians. Each of these has a role of creative service to the truth; none can be considered as having a juridical power to stifle or invalidate the other. Rather, each magisterium must be seen as open to the corrective influence of the other magisteria.[61]

Each of these very real aspects of the Church's teaching function must be seen in relation to the other; it is only together that they fulfill the purpose of a Christian community that teaches. For it is only together, acting in harmony, that they allow the Church to proclaim the presence of God's kingdom, initiated by Jesus in his teaching. It is only as a balanced reality of the Church's life that its teaching function is able to present the Church as that eschatological reality chosen by God to effect his reign as proclaimed by Jesus. Insofar as the Church witnesses to the reign of God as a proclaimed reality in Jesus, it effects that reign. Thus the teaching function of the Church is determined and directed by the *eschaton* towards which it points and from which it comes.[62] It is only in this totality that the Church can teach; any imbalance or neglect of this essential note of wholeness degrades and reduces its teaching function to the point that it no longer is a witness to God's kingdom as proclaimed by Jesus, but rather speaks with 'stammering lips'.[63] The unity of authority must give way to the freedom of diversity, for it is thus that Jesus announced the kingdom of God.

61. D. Maguire, 'Morality and Magisterium' in *Cross Currents* 18 (1968) pp. 62–3.
62. J. McKenzie, *The Power and the Wisdom,* p. 69; see also K. Rahner, 'Lehramt' in *L. Th.K.,* vol. 6, pp. 889–90.
63. J. H. Newman, *V.M.* II, p. 271.

Appendix

I

The following letter, written by Newman to W. Monsell (later Lord Emly) on 13 January 1863, is a fine illustration of how the Rambler *affair continued to rankle him. Notice also his presentation of how the Church sifts and chooses, proves and solidifies its theological opinions. This freedom of discussion and thought, within its limits, of the whole Church, Newman had felt to be essential to its task in the modern world and it was one of the major principles he was fighting for with the* Rambler. *But even in this case he does not countenance going against the Church's authority; God's providence will out in the end.*

I will tell you what seems to me to be the real grievance:—viz. that in this generation the Bishops should pass such grave matter, (to use the Oxford term) by *cumulation*. The wisdom of the Church has provided many courts for theological questions, one higher than another. I suppose, in the middle ages, (which have a manliness and boldness, of which now there is no great lack) a question was first debated in a University, then in one University against another, or by one order of friars against another;—then perhaps it came before a theological faculty; then it went to the Metropolitan; and so by various stages and through many examinations and judgments, it came before the Holy See. But now, what do the Bishops do? All courts are superseded, because the whole English-speaking Catholic population all over the world is under Propaganda, an arbitrary, military power. Propaganda is our only court of appeal; but to it the Bishops go, and secure it and commit it, before they move one step in the matter which calls for interference. And how is Propaganda to know anything about an English controversy, since it talks Italian? by extempore translations (I do not speak at random) or the ex parte assertion of some narrow minded Bishop, though he may be saintly too. And who is Propaganda? virtually, one sharp man of business, who works day and night, and dispatches his work quick off, to the East and the West; a high dignitary indeed, perhaps an Archbishop, but after all little more than a clerk, or (according to his name) a Secretary, and two or three clerks under him. In this age at least, Quantula sapientia regimur!

Well, if all this could be said of any human institution, I should feel very indignant; but it is the very sense and certainty I have of the Church being divine, which at once makes it easy to bear. All this will be overruled; it may lead to much temporary mischief, but it will be overruled. And we do not make things better by disobedience. We may be able indeed to complicate matters, and to delay the necessary reforms; but our part is obedience. If we are but patient, all will come right.

[in *Orat.*, vol. 36]

2

In a memorandum dated 14 January 1860, Newman lets out all the bile and bitterness that had been building up in him, which finally came to a head with the shoddy handling accorded him in the Rambler *affair (see ch. 11, above).*

All through life things happen to me which do not happen to others—I am a scapegoat. It was a Cardinal who got off in the

Achilli matter, while I suffered, or Doellinger gets off not I. It was on occasion of that Achilli matter that I anticipated what is taking place now. On looking back to my life, I find myself as... Sisyphus, rolling my load up the hill for ten years and never cresting it, but falling back. Thus I failed in the schools in 1820; then I slowly mended things and built myself into somebody with a prospect of something till 1830, and then on the 5th May I had to retire from College Office and was nobody again. Then again I set to work and by 1840 had become somebody once more, when on February 27, No. 90 was attacked, and down I fell again. Then slowly I went on and by 1850 I had as a Catholic so recovered my ground that the Pope made me a D.D., when on July 28, 1851 I delivered the lecture in the Corn Exchange, which delivered me over into the hands of Achilli. On that occasion I said to several persons . . . in another 10 years I shall be had up before Rome.

[in *Orat.*, vol. 35]

3

Before the controversy began which ended in the Apologia, *Newman had written a semi-translation of the Munich Brief, together with a running commentary. (The whole of it is now to be found in* Ward I, *pp. 641–2.) One section is of particular importance in ascertaining his views on papal authority. The Brief states (Denzinger*[31]*, n. 1684):*

Sed cum agatur de illa subiectione, qua ex conscientia ii omnes catholici obstringuntur, qui in contemplatrices scientias incumbunt, ut novas suis scriptis Ecclesiae afferant utilitates, idcirco eiusdem conventus viri recognoscere debent, sapientibus catholicis haud satis esse, ut praefata Ecclesiae dogmata recipiant ac venerentur, verum etiam opus esse, ut se subiciant decisionibus, quae ad doctrinam pertinentes a Pontificiis Congregationibus proferuntur, tum iis doctrinae capitibus, quae communi et constanti Catholicorum consensu retinentur ut theologicae veritates et conclusiones ita certae, ut opiniones eisdem doctrinae capitibus adversae quamquam haereticae dici nequeant, tamen aliam theologicam mereantur censuram.

Newman then comments:

I thought it was commonly said that Galileo's fault was that he meddled with *theology,* and that, if he had confined himself to *scientific conclusions* he would have been let alone; but surely the language of the Brief here and before is as if even men of science must keep theological conclusions before them in treating of science. Well, I am not likely to investigate in science, but I certainly could not write a word upon the special controversies and difficulties of the day with a view to defend religion from free thinking physicists without allowing them freedom of logic in their own science; so that, if I understand this Brief, it is simply a providential intimation to every religious man, that, at this moment, we are simply to be silent while scientific investigation proceeds—and say not a word on questions of interpretation of Scripture, etc., etc. when perplexed persons ask us—and I am not sure that it will not prove to be the best course.

4

A letter dated 9 November 1865 illustrates quite clearly what Newman understood by the schola theologorum. *In his schema, it is supremely representative of the action taken by the whole Church in deciding its witness. The letter is to be found in the Birmingham Archives, in 'Cardinal Newman's Papers on Infallibility', edited and transcribed by H. Tristram, pp. 52–4:*

By the *schola* I mean a generalization for the decisions of theologians throughout the world. And as in all matters, and not the least in intellectual, there is a natural tendency to collect into centres, the *schola* is in fact a generalized name for the bodies of theologians throughout the world, or for the schools of the Church viewed as a whole . . . The first great schools . . . are nearly all destroyed in consequence of the revolutions which ushered in this century. This has been a serious evil, as it throws us back on the Roman school, as nearly the only school in the Church . . . The *schola* answers many purposes. It defends the dogma, and articulates it. Further than this, since its teaching is far wider than the Apostolic dogma which is *de fide*, it protects it as forming a large body of doctrine which must be got through before an attack can be made on the dogma. And it steadies the opinion of the Church, embodying tradition, and hindering frequent changes. And it is the arena in which questions of development and change are argued out. And again, if changes of opinion are to come, and false interpretations of scripture, or false views of the dogma, to be set right, it prepares the way, accustoming the minds of Catholics to the idea of the change, and preventing surprise and scandal . . . Without it, the dogma of the Church would be the raw flesh without skin; nay, or a tree without leaves; for as devotional feelings clothe the dogma on the one hand, so does the teaching of the *schola* on the other. Moreover, it is the immediate authority for the practical working and course of the Church, e.g. what are mortal sins, what venial, what are the effects of the Mass, what about Indulgences, etc., etc.?

5

The following letter was written by Newman to Bishop Ullathorne during the Vatican Council. It was meant as strictly private, but through some way as yet not fully explained, the letter got out and was soon published in papers ranging the breadth of Europe. Newman was eventually happy that it had gotten out, for in this manner his mind became known, through no fault of his own, to a much wider public.

I thank your Lordship very heartily for your most interesting and seasonable letter. Such letters (if they could be circulated) would do much to re-assure the many minds which are at present disturbed when they look towards Rome. Rome ought to be a name to lighten the heart at all times, and a Council's proper office is, when some great heresy or other evil impends, to inspire the faithful with hope and confidence. But now we have the greatest meeting which has ever been, and that in Rome, infusing into us by the accredited organs of Rome (such as the *Civiltà,* the *Armonia,* the *Univers,* and the *Tablet*) little else than fear and dismay. Where we are all at rest and have no doubts, and, at least practically, not to say doctrinally, hold the Holy Father to be infallible, suddenly there is thunder in the clear sky, and we are told to prepare for something, we know not what, to try our faith, we know not how. No impending danger is to be averted but a great difficulty is to be created. Is this the proper work for an Ecumenical Council? As to myself personally, please God, I do not expect any trial at all, but I cannot help suffering with the various souls that are suffering. I look with anxiety at the prospect of having to defend decisions which may not be difficult to my private judgment, but may be most difficult to defend logically in the face of historical facts. What have we done to be treated as the Faithful never were treated before? When has definition of doctrine *de fide* been a luxury of devotion and not a stern painful necessity? Why should an aggressive and insolent faction be allowed to make the hearts of the just mourn whom the Lord hath not made sorrowful? Why can't we be let alone when we have pursued peace and thought no evil? I assure you, my dear Lord, some of the truest minds are driven one way and another, and do not know where to rest their feet; one day determining to give up all theology as a bad job and recklessly to believe henceforth almost that the Pope is impeccable; at another tempted to believe all the worst that a book like Janus says; at another doubting about the capacity possessed by Bishops drawn from all corners of the earth to judge what is fitting for European society, and then again angry with the Holy See for listening to the flattery of a clique of Jesuits, Redemptorists and Converts. Then again think of the score of Pontifical scandals in the history of eighteen centuries which have partly been poured out, and partly are still to come out. What Murphy inflicted upon us in one way, M. Veuillot is indirectly bringing on us in another. And then again the blight which is falling upon the multitude of Anglican ritualists, who themselves perhaps, or at least their leaders, may never become Catholics, but who are leavening the various English parties and denominations (far beyond their range) with principles and sentiments tending towards their ultimate adoption into the Catholic Church.

With these thoughts before me, I am continually asking myself whether I ought not to make my feelings public; but all I do is to pray those great early Doctors of the Church, whose intercession would decide the matter,—Augustine and the rest,—to avert so great a calamity. If it is God's Will that the Pope's Infallibility should be defined, then it is His Blessed Will to throw back the times and the moments of that triumph He has destined for His Kingdom; and I shall feel I have to bow my head to His Adorable Inscrutable Providence . . .

[in *Ward* II, pp. 287–8]

6

In writing to A. Plummer, a young Anglican clergyman who had studied in Munich, Newman often came to talk of Döllinger and his reaction to the Council. In this letter he more clearly defines what exactly papal infallibility entails, and what the future can hold; in this regard, his anticipation of Vatican II is startling, to say the least. Newman begins by taking up Döllinger's charge that the Council had founded its definition on an erroneous interpretation of Scripture:

But I thought it was a great principle of theology, that all that was divinely guaranteed in a Council was the truth of its resulting decision . . . I had always thought, and I think still, that the infallibility of the Church is an *inference* (a necessary inference) from her prerogative that she is the divinely appointed Teacher of her children, and of the world. She cannot fulfill this office *without* divine help—that is, she never can be *permitted to go wrong* in the truths of revelation. This a negative proposition; the very idea of infallibility is a negative. She teaches by human means, she ascertains the truth by human means—of course assisted by grace, but so is every inquirer; and she has *in kind* no promise of invincible grace which a Father or divine, or an inquirer has not. But she has this security, that, *in order* to fulfill her office, her *outcome* is always true in the matter of revelation. She is not inspired—the word has sometimes been used, and in Councils especially—but, properly speaking, inspiration is positive, and infallibility is negative; and a definition may be absolute truth, though the grounds suggested for it in the definition, the texts, the patristic authorities, the historical passages, are all mistakes. In saying this, I think I speak with Bellarmine and Fr Perrone. Perhaps I am used to only one school of theology, but I never heard of any view besides that which I am drawing out . . . I do not know where we should be, if our fundamental principle were not, that the ultimate enunciations, the upshot and outcome of the Church's deliberations, are certainly true. Of course, it is quite fair to say that this or that Council is not legitimate. This is a question of fact, viz. whether or not the Church has spoken . . . looking at early history, it would seem as if the Church moved on to the perfect truth by various successive declarations, alternately in contrary directions, and thus perfecting, completing, supplying each other. Let us have a little faith in her I say. Pius is not the last of the Popes. The 4th Council modified the 3rd, the 5th the 4th . . . The late definition does not so much need to be undone, as to be completed. It needs *safeguards* to the Pope's possible acts—explanations as to the matter and extent of his power. I know that a violent reckless party, had it its will, would at this moment define that the Pope's power needs no safeguards, no explanations; but there is a limit to the triumph of the tyrannical. Let us be patient, let us have faith, and a new Pope, and a re-assembled Council may trim the boat.

[in *Plummer,* second packet, 3 April 1871; also in F. ·L. Cross, *J. H. Newman,* pp. 168–70]

Bibliography

1. The Published Works of John Henry Newman:

Unless otherwise noted, the edition used is that of Longmans, London. The date immediately following a given volume is that of its first publication; the date in parentheses is that of the edition used in the present work.

An Essay in Aid of a Grammar of Assent, 1870 (1901).

An Essay on the Development of Christian Doctrine, 1845 (New York: Doubleday & Co., 1960).

'An Unpublished Paper by Cardinal Newman on the Development of Doctrine' (the so-called 'Flanagan Letter'), H. M. Achaval ed., in *Gregorianum* 39 (1958) 585–96; also to be found in *Journal of Theological Studies*, October 1958, pp. 324–35, C. S. Dessain ed.

Apologia pro Vita Sua, first edition 1864 (cited according to the edition of Doubleday & Co., New York, 1956); second edition 1865 (1908). Unless otherwise stated, it is cited according to the second edition.

Autobiographical Writings, H. Tristram ed. and introduction, New York: Sheed & Ward, 1956.

Callista, a Sketch of the Third Century, 1855 (Westminister, Maryland: Newman Press, 1962).

'Cardinal Newman's Theses de fide and his proposed Introduction to the French Translation of the University Sermons', H. Tristram ed., in *Gregorianum* 18 (1937) 219–60.

Catholic Sermons of Cardinal Newman, edited by the Fathers of the Birmingham Oratory, London: Burns & Oates, 1957.

Certain Difficulties felt by Anglicans in Catholic Teaching, vol. 1, 1850 (1897); vol. 2, 1865–74 (1900).

Discourses Addressed to Mixed Congregations, 1849 (1899).

Discussions and Arguments, 1872 (1918).

Essays Critical and Historical, vol. 1, 1871 (1901); vol. 2, 1871 (London: Pickering, 1871).

Fifteen Sermons Preached before the University of Oxford, 1843 (1900).

Historical Sketches, vol. 1, 1872 (1891); vol. 2, 1872 (1891); vol. 3, 1856–72 (1899).

Lectures on Justification, 1838 (1900).

Lectures on the Present Position of Catholics in England, 1851 (1899).

Loss and Gain, 1848 (London: Burns & Oates, 1962).

Meditations and Devotions, 1893 (1901).

'On Consulting the Faithful in Matters of Doctrine' in the *Rambler,* July 1859, pp. 198–230 (also John Coulson ed. and introduction, London: Chapman, 1961).

On the Inspiration of Scripture, J. D. Holmes and R. Murray sj ed. and introduction, London, 1967.

Parochial and Plain Sermons, vol. 1, 1834 (1898); vol. 2, 1835 (1891); vol. 3, 1836 (1901); vol. 4, 1839 (1900); vol. 5, 1840 (1901); vol. 6, 1842 (1891); vol. 7, 1842–43 (1891); vol. 8, 1842–43 (1891).

Select Treatises of St. Athanasius, 1841–44; 1887 (1900).

Sermons bearing on Subjects of the Day, 1843 (1898).

Sermon Notes of J. H. Cardinal Newman, 1849–78, London, 1914².

Sermons preached on Various Occasions, 1857 (1900).

Stray Essays on Controversial Points, privately printed in Birmingham, 1890.

The Arians of the Fourth Century, 1833 (1901; unless otherwise stated it is cited according to the third edition of 1871).

The Idea of a University, 1852 (1901).

'The Newman-Perrone Paper on Development' in *Gregorianum* 16 (1935) 402–47 (originally *De catholici dogmatis evolutione,* written in 1847).

The Via Media of the Anglican Church, vol. 1, 1830–41 (1901); vol. 2, 1830–41 (1899).

Tracts for the Times, London, vol. 1, 1833–34 (1840); vol. 2, p. 1, 1834–35 (1840); vol. 2, p. 2, 1834–35 (1842); vol. 3, 1835–36 (1840); vol. 4, 1836–37 (1840); vol. 5, 1838–40 (1840). Newman edited some of these; others he helped write. The following, with the exception of n. 15, were composed entirely by him: n. 1: Thoughts on the Ministerial Commission; n. 2: The Catholic Church; n. 3: Thoughts respectively addressed to the Clergy on Alterations in the Liturgy; n. 6: The Present Obligation of Primitive Practice; n. 7: The Episcopal Church Apostolical; n. 8: The Gospel a Law of Liberty; n. 10: Heads of a Weekday Lecture delivered to a Country Congregation; n. 11: The Visible Church, Letters 1 and 2; n. 15: (together with Palmer) On the Apostolic Succession of the English Church; n. 19: On Arguing concerning the Apostolic Succession; n. 20: The same continued; n. 21: Mortification of the Flesh a Scripture Duty; n. 31: The Reformed Church; n. 33: Primitive Episcopacy; n. 34: Rites and Customs of the Church; n. 38: Via Media, n. 1; n. 41: Via Media, n. 2 (together with n. 38 to be found in: *V.M.* II, pp. 19–48); n. 45: The Grounds of our Faith; n. 47: The Visible Church, Letter 4; n. 71: Against Romanism, n. 1 (in *V.M.* II, pp. 95–141); n. 73: On the Introduction of Rationalistic Principles into Religion (in *Ess. C.H.* I, pp. 30–95); n. 74: Catena Patrum, n. 1, Testimony of Anglican Divines re Apostolic Succession; n. 79: On Purgatory; n. 82: Letter to a Magazine re Pusey's Tract on Baptism (in *V.M.* II, pp. 143–94); n. 83: Advent Sermons on Antichrist (in *Dis. and Arg.*, pp. 44–108); n. 85: Lectures on the Scripture Proofs of the Doctrines of the Church (in *Dis. and Arg.*, pp. 109–253); n. 88: The Greek Devotions of Bishop Andrews Translated and Arranged; n. 90: Remarks on certain Passages of the 39 Articles (this was not published in the 5th volume of the collected tracts, but is to be found in *V.M.* II, pp. 259–348).

Tracts Theological and Ecclesiastical, 1874 (1899).
Two Essays on Biblical and on Ecclesiastical Miracles, 1825–43 (1901).
Verses on Various Occasions, 1867 (1900).

2. The Published Letters and Diaries of John Henry Newman:

Dessain, C. S., ed., *The Letters and Diaries of John Henry Newman*, London, 1961ff, vol. 11. Littlemore to Rome, October 1845–December 1846; vol. 12, Rome to Birmingham, January 1847–December 1848; vol. 13, Birmingham and London, January 1849–June 1850; vol. 14, Papal Aggression, July 1850–December 1851; vol. 15, The Achilli Trial, January 1852–December 1853; vol. 16, Founding a University, January 1854–September 1855.

Harper, G. H., ed., *Cardinal Newman and William Froude, F.R.S.: a Correspondence*, Baltimore, 1933.

Mozley, Anne, ed., *Letters and Correspondence of J. H. Newman during his Life in the English Church*, 2 volumes, London, 1890 (1898²).

Mozley, Dorothea, ed., *Newman Family Letters*, London, 1962.

The Oratory Fathers, ed., *Correspondence of John H. Newman with John Keble and Others: 1839–45*, London, 1917.

3. Unpublished Letters and Papers:

Abbé Jager–Benjamin Harrison–J. H. Newman, *Correspondence*, vol. 18 of the Newman papers at the Oratory, Birmingham.

J. H. Newman, *Correspondence on the Rambler Affair*, volumes 33–36 of the Newman papers at the Oratory, Birmingham.

J. H. Newman, *Cardinal Newman's Papers on Infallibility, 1866–68,* typed, compiled and introduced by H. Tristram, in manuscript: 105 pages. The originals under file: B.7.4.

J. H. Newman, *Vatican I Correspondence:* volumes 44–47 of the Newman papers at the Oratory, Birmingham.

J. H. Newman–Duke of Norfolk, *Correspondence:* vol. 48 (October–7 December 1874); vol. 49 (7 December 1874–1875); vol. 50 (January–February 1875); vol. 51 (March–December 1875) of the Newman papers at the Oratory, Birmingham.

J. H. Newman–A. Plummer, *Correspondence:* 1) 21 letters from J. H. Newman to A. Plummer, 1870–74; 2) 21 letters from J. H. Newman to A. Plummer 1875–88; located in the Plummer papers at Pusey House, Oxford.

4.   Books, both on Newman and on the Problematic in General:

Atholz, J. L., *The Liberal Catholic Movement in England: The 'Rambler' and its Contributors,* London, 1962.

Bainvel, J. V., *De Magisterio vivo et de Traditione,* Paris, 1905.

Bartz, W., *Die lehrende Kirche,* Trier, 1959.

Biemer, Günter, *Die Lehre von der Tradition nach John Henry Newman,* diss. masch., Tübingen, 1959; published as *Ueberlieferung und Offenbarung,* Freiburg, 1961; English translation, *Newman on Tradition,* New York, 1967.

Bouyer, Louis, *Newman: his Life and Spirituality,* London, 1958.

Butler, Dom Cuthbert, *The Vatican Council: 1869–1870,* London, 1962.

Cameron, J. M., *John Henry Newman,* London, 1963.

Chadwick, Owen, *From Boussuet to Newman: The Idea of Doctrinal Development,* Cambridge, 1957.

Chadwick, Owen, *The Victorian Church,* Part I, London, 1966.

Church, R. W., *The Oxford Movement: Twelve Years: 1833–45,* London, 1922[3].

Congar, Yves, OP, *Lay People in the Church,* translated by D. Attwater, Westminister, Maryland, 1962[2].

Conolly, M., *Newman's Anglican Concept of the Doctrinal Authority of the Church and its Relation to Infallibility,* Rome, 1938.

Cross, F. L., *John Henry Newman,* Glasgow, 1933.

Cross, F. L., ed., *Oxford Dictionary of the Christian Church,* London, 1958[2].

Davis, Charles, *A Question of Conscience,* London, 1967.

Dessain, C. S., *John Henry Newman,* London, 1964.

Dibble, R. A., *John Henry Newman: The Concept of Infallible Doctrinal Authority,* Washington, 1955.

Elliot-Binns, L. E., *The Development of English Theology in the Later Nineteenth Century*, London, 1952.

Fecker, F., *Kardinal Newman und sein Weg zur Kirche*, Munich-Gladbach, 1914.

Femiano, Samuel, *Infallibility of the Laity: The Legacy of Newman*, New York, 1967.

Gladstone, W. E., *The Vatican Decrees in Their Bearing on Civil Allegiance. A Political Expostulation*, London, 1874.

Greenfield, Robert H., *The Attitude of the Tractarians to the Roman Catholic Church: 1833–1850*, Oxford, 1956.

Guitton, Jean, *Mitbürgern der Wahrheit. Das Zeugnis der Laien in Fragen der Glaubenslehre*, Salzburg, 1964; English translation, *The Church and the Laity: From Newman to Vatican II*, New York, 1965.

Hammans, H., *Die neueren Erklärungen der Dogmenentwicklung*, Essen, 1965.

Jager, Abbé Jean-N., *Le Protestantisme aux prises avec le Catholicisme*, Paris, 1836[2].

Keble, John, *National Apostasy: Considered in a Sermon Preached in St. Mary's, Oxford, Brfore the Judges of Assize, Sunday, July 14, 1833*, Oxford, 1833.

Laepple, Alfred, *Der Einzelne in der Kirche. Wesenszüge einer Theologie des Einzelnen nach John Henry Kardinal Newman*, Teil I., Munich, 1952.

Laros, M., *John Henry Newman*, Leipzig, 1920.

MacDougall, Hugh, OMI, *The Acton–Newman Relations. The Dilemma of Christian Liberalism*, New York, 1962.

McKenzie, John L., SJ, *Authority in the Church*, New York, 1966.

Mann, Joseph, *John Henry Newman als Kerygmatiker*, Leipzig, 1965.

Moody, John, *John Henry Newman*, New York, 1945.

O'Dwyer, E. T., *Cardinal Newman and the Encyclical Pascendi: An Essay*, London, 1908[2].

Patterson, W. T., *The Laity and the Teaching Church, According to J. H. Newman*, Rome, 1959.

Perrone, J., *Praelectiones theologicae*, Rome, 1841[2].

Prior, J., *Cardinal Newman and the Infallibility of the Church*, Rome, 1909.

Quinn, J. R., *The Recognition of the True Church According to John Henry Newman*, Washington, 1954.

Rich, Edward C., *Spiritual Authority in the Church of England*, London, 1953.

Rickaby, Joseph, SJ, *Index to the Works of John Henry Cardinal Newman*, London, 1914.

Schiffers, N., *Die Einheit der Kirche nach J. H. Newman*, Düsseldorf, 1956.

Schmaus, Michael, *Katholische Dogmatik*, Bd. III, 1, Munich, 1958.

Seynaeve, Jaak, *Cardinal Newman's Doctrine on Holy Scripture, According* to His Published Works and Previously Unedited Manuscripts, Louvain, 1953.

Söhngen, Gottlieb, *Die Einheit in der Theologie*, Munich, 1952.

Stangl, F. S., J. H. *Newman's Doctrine of Papal Infallibility in the Gladstone Controversy*, Rome, 1962.

Thureau-Dangin, Paul, *La Renaissance Catholique en Angleterre*, 3 volumes, Paris, 1906.

Trevor, M., *Newman*, London, 1961, 2 volumes.

Van de Pol, W. H., *Die Kirche im Leben und Denken Newmans*, Salzburg-Leipzig, 1937.

Walgrave, J. H., *Newman as Theologian*, London, 1960.

Ward, Maisie, *Young Mr. Newman*, London, 1952.

Ward, Wilfrid, *The Life of John Henry Cardinal Newman*, 2 volumes, London, 1912.

5. Articles both on Newman and on the Problematic in General:

Adolphs, R., in *The National Catholic Reporter*, Kansas City, 23 August 1967, p. 10.

Bacchus, F. and Tristram, H., 'Newman' in *Dictionnaire de théologie catholique*, vol. 11, Paris, 1931, pp. 353–97.

Bastnagel, C., 'Authority of Papal Encyclicals' in *Catholic Educational Review*, March, 1930, pp. 166–9.

Baum, Gregory, 'The Magisterium in a Changing Church' in *Concilium* 3 (January 1967) pp. 34–42.

Becker, W., 'John Henry Kardinal Newman' in *Lexikon für Theologie und Kirche*, vol. 7, Freiburg, 1962, pp. 932–6.

Becker, W., 'Newman und die Kirche' in *Newman Studien* I, pp. 236–47.

Beumer, J., 'Das authentische Lehramt der Kirche' in *Theologie und Glauben Werkheft*, 1948, pp. 272–87.

Biemer, Günter, 'Die doppelte Suffizienz der Glaubensquellen und ihre Bedeutung nach Kardinal Newman' in *Tübinger theologische Quartalschrift* 140 (1960) 385–409.

Biemer, G., 'Newman an das Vaticanum II' in *Wort und Wahrheit* 16 (1961) 409–19.

Biemer, G., 'Traditio et Scriptura iuxta Anglicanos et Cardinalem Newman' in *De Scriptura et Traditione*, Rome, 1963, pp. 573–87.

Biemer, G., 'Ueber die Schriftlesung nach Kardinal Newman' in *Oberrheinisches Pastoralblatt* 62 (1961) 22–6.

Burke, W. P., 'The Ancient Newness of Dogma' in *The American Ecclesiastical Review* 115 (1946) 169–85.

Chenu, Marie-Dominique, OP, 'Theology as an Ecclesial Science' in *Concilium* 1 (January 1967) 47–52.

Congar, Yves, 'L'écclésiologie de la Révolution française au Concile du Vatican, sous le signe de l'affirmation de l'autorité' in *L'Ecclésiologie au XIXe siècle,* Paris, 1960, pp. 77–114.

Cox, Harvey, 'Revolt in the Church' in *Playboy,* January 1967, pp. 129ff.

Davis, Charles, 'Why I Left the Roman Catholic Church' in *The Observer Review,* 1 January 1967, p. 1.

Davis, H. F., 'Newman, the Bible, and the obiter dicta' in *The Life of the Spirit* 8 (1954) 398–407.

Davis, H. F., 'Newman, the Individual and the Church' in *Blackfriars* 39 (1958) 310–21.

Davis, H. F., 'The Catholicism of Cardinal Newman' in *J. H. Newman: Centenary Essays,* H. Tristram ed., London, 1945, pp. 36–54.

Davis, H. F., 'Le rôle et l'apostolat de la hiérarchie et du laicat dans la théologie de l'Eglise chez Newman' in *L'Ecclésiologie au XIXe siècle,* Paris, 1960, pp. 329–49.

Dessain, C. S., 'Cardinal Newman and Ecumenism' in *The Clergy Review* 50 (1965) 119–37, 189–206.

Dessain, C. S., 'Cardinal Newman on the Laity' in *The Life of the Spirit* 16 (1961) 51–62.

Dessain, C. S., 'The Newman Archive of Birmingham' in *Newman Studien* III, Nuremberg, 1957, pp. 269–73.

Dessain, C. S., 'What Newman Taught in Manning's Church' in *Infallibility in the Church and Anglican-Catholic Dialogue,* A. M. Farrer et al., London, 1968.

Drinkwater, Canon F. H., 'Ordinary and Universal' in *The Clergy Review* 50 (January 1965) 2–22.

Fenton, Joseph C., 'Newman and Papal Infallibility' in *American Essays for the Newman Centenial,* J. Ryan and E. Bernard ed., Washington, 1947.

Fenton, Joseph C., 'The Doctrinal Authority of Papal Encyclicals' in *The American Ecclesiastical Review* 118 (1949) 136–50, 210–20.

Fenton, Joseph C., 'The Necessity for the Definition of Papal Infallibility by the Vatican Council' in *The American Ecclesiastical Review* 115 (1946) 439–57.

Fries, Heinrich, 'Die Dogmengeschichte des fünften Jahrhunderts im theologischen Werdegang von J. H. Newman' in *Das Konzil von Chalkedon,* A. Grillmeier und H. Bacht ed., Würzburg, 1954, vol. 3, pp. 421–54.

Fries, Heinrich, 'Newman und Döllinger' in *Newman Studien* I, pp. 29–76.

Fries, Heinrich, 'Newmans Bedeutung für die Theologie' in *Newman Studien* I, pp. 181–98.

Fries, Heinrich, 'J. H. Newmans Beitrag zum Verständnis der Tradition' in *Die mündliche Ueberlieferung,* M. Schmaus ed., Munich, 1957.

Gregory, T. S., 'Newman and Liberalism' in *A Tribute to Newman,* M. Tierney ed., Dublin, 1945, pp. 84–115.

H., W. S., 'Le sens ecclesial de Newman' in *Dictionnaire de Spiritualité,* vol. 4, Paris, 1960, pp. 433–6.

Healy, J., 'Cardinal Newman on the Inspiration of Scripture' in *The Irish Ecclesiastical Record,* 1884, pp. 137–49.

Heron, S., 'Newman and the Roman Church' in *Theology Today* 15 (1959) 389–90.

Hollis, Christopher, 'Cardinal Newman and Dean Church' in *J. H. Newman: Centenary Essays,* H. Tristram ed., London, 1945, pp. 68–91.

Johnson, H. J. T., 'Leo XIII, Cardinal Newman and the Inerrancy of Scripture' in *Downside Review* 69 (1950) 411–27.

Johnson, H. J. T., 'The Controversy Between Newman and Gladstone Over the Question of Civil Allegiance' in *Dublin Review* 217 (October 1945) 173–81.

Karrer, Otto, 'John Henry Newman' in *Hochland* 40 (1947/48) 514–38.

Karrer, Otto, 'J. H. Newman, Bekenner der Autorität und der christlichen Freiheit. Unser Weg' in *Schweizer katholisches Jugendblatt* 5/6 (1956) 60–65.

Karrer, Otto, 'Newmans Weg in die Kirche und sein Weg in der Kirche' in *Sentire Ecclesiam,* Jean Daniélou und Herbert Vorgrimler ed., Freiburg, 1961, pp. 676–742.

Laros, M., 'Autorität und Gewissen' in *Hochland* 36 (1938/39) 265–80.

Laros, M., 'Kardinal Newman und das "Neue Dogma"' in *Die Neue Ordnung* 5 (1951) 6–26.

Laros, M., 'Laie und Lehramt in der Kirche' in *Hochland* 37 (1939–40) 45–54.

Martinit, Winifried, 'Newman oder Manning?' in *Hochland* 40 (1947/48) 186–8.

Murray, J. Courtney, SJ, in *The National Catholic Reporter* 17 May 1967, p. 3.

Nicholls, David, 'Newman's Anglican Critics' in *Anglican Theological Review* 47 (October 1965) 377–95.

O'Flynn, J. A., 'Newman and the Scripture' in *Irish Theological Quarterly* 21 (1954) 264–9.

Roesch, R., SM, in *The National Catholic Reporter,* 4 April 1967, p. 5.

Schiffers, N., 'Schrift und Tradition bei J. H. Newman' in *Schrift und Tradition,* die deutsche Arbeitsgemeinschaft für Mariologie ed., Essen, 1962, pp. 250–66.

Stephenson, A. A., 'Cardinal Newman and the Development of Doctrine' in *Journal of Ecumenical Studies* 3 (1966) 463–85.

Stern, Jean, 'La Controverse de Newman avec L'Abbé Jager et la Théorie du Développement' in *Newman Studien* 6 (1963) 123–42.

Stern, J., 'Traditions apostoliques et Magistère selon J. H. Newman' in *Revue des sciences philosophiques et théologiques* 47 (1963) 35–57.

Tristram, H., 'In the lists with the Abbé Jager' in *J. H. Newman: Centenary Essays,* H. Tristram ed., London, 1945.

Tristram, H. and Bacchus, F., 'Newman' in *Dictionnaire de théologie catholique,* vol. 11, Paris, 1931, pp. 353–97.

Tristram, H., 'Newman Looked for Well-Instructed Laity' in *The Advocate* 78 (1945).

Tristram, H., 'Cardinal Newman and Baron von Hügel' in *The Dublin Review* 509 (1966) 295–302.

Tristram, H., 'On Reading Newman' in *J. H. Newman: Centenary Essays,* H. Tristram ed., London, 1945, pp. 223–41.

Weigel, Gustave, sj, 'Significance of Papal Announcements' in *The Papal Encyclicals in their Historical Context,* Anne Freemantle ed., New York, 1963, pp. 9–20.

Willam, F. M., 'J. H. Newman und P. Perrone' in *Newman Studien* 2, pp. 120–45.

Willam, F. M., 'Kardinal Newman und das erste vatikanische Konzil' in *Orientierung* 26 (1962) 174–8.

Willam, F. M., 'Kardinal J. H. Newman und die kirchliche Lehrtradition' in *Orientierung* 22 (1958) 61–66.

Willam, F. M., 'Newman vor 1871 über Primat und Episkopat' in *Orientierung* 27 (1963) 162–4.

Index